KIDNEY DISEASE DIET FOR SENIORS ON STAGE 3

Easy Low-Sodium, Low-Potassium Recipes and Gentle Exercises to Support Renal Function and Kidney-Health:

A Complete Guide for Managing CKD

Matthew Brooks

Copyright © 2024 by Matthew Brooks

All rights reserved.

No part of this book may be reproduced, distributed, or transmitted in any form or by any means, including photocopying, recording, or other electronic or mechanical methods, without the prior written permission of the author, except in the case of brief quotations embodied in reviews and certain other non-commercial uses permitted by copyright law.

Disclaimer

This book is for informational and educational purposes only. The author and publisher are not medical professionals and are not offering medical advice. Please consult your healthcare provider before starting any new diet, exercise program, or treatment. The recipes and exercises provided in this book are intended for general use and may not be suitable for all individuals. The author and publisher are not responsible for any adverse effects resulting from the use of the information provided herein.

Table of Contents

INTRODUCTION 5
Chapter 1: UNDERSTANDING KIDNEY DISEASE & NUTRITION 10
Chapter 2: THE KIDNEY-FRIENDLY DIET 20
Chapter 3: SETTING UP YOUR KITCHEN FOR KIDNEY HEALTH 31
Chapter 4: BREAKFASTS TO START THE DAY RIGHT 36
Chapter 5: ENERGIZING LUNCHES 54
Chapter 6: SATISFYING DINNERS 76
Chapter 7: WHOLESOME SIDES AND SNACKS 99
Chapter 8: GUILT-FREE DESSERTS AND SWEET TREATS 118
Chapter 9: HYDRATION AND BEVERAGES RECIPES 140
Chapter 11: KIDNEY-FRIENDLY AIR FRYER RECIPES 150
Chapter 12: MEAL PLANNING & BATCH COOKING 160
Chapter 10: CAREGIVER TIPS AND SUPPORT FOR FAMILY MEMBERS ... 183
Chapter 11: GENTLE EXERCISE FOR KIDNEY HEALTH 187
Chapter 12: MAINTAINING A POSITIVE MINDSET & REDUCING STRESS 191
Kidney Diet Myths That Could Be Harming You 194
CONCLUSION 199
Bonus 202
Recipes Index 211

INTRODUCTION

Welcome! If you've picked up this book, chances are you or someone close to you is navigating the challenges of kidney disease. You might feel overwhelmed, uncertain, and perhaps even a bit scared about what lies ahead. Trust me, you're not alone in this. I've walked this path myself when my wife was diagnosed with chronic kidney disease. It was a journey filled with twists and turns, one where each day brought new questions, but also new opportunities to make a difference in her health and well-being.

I remember the day we sat in that cold, sterile doctor's office, the weight of her diagnosis hitting us like a ton of bricks. Stage 3 Chronic Kidney Disease sounded daunting, and all I could think was, *How could I help her? How could we manage this?* Our Lives changed over the next few months. Our meals, once filled with her favorite flavors and comfort foods, needed an overhaul. We quickly discovered that what she ate could make a huge difference in how she felt each day, but figuring out what was safe and nourishing for her kidneys felt like navigating a maze.

I started by researching everything I could about kidney disease nutrition. I was determined not to let this diagnosis define her life or our relationship with food. I wanted our meals to still bring us together, to provide comfort and health rather than fear and restriction. But there was so much conflicting information out there. So many "kidney-friendly" cookbooks and resources seemed repetitive, or they missed the mark in addressing the unique needs of seniors like my wife, who needed meals that weren't just healthy but were easy, practical, and enjoyable.

One of the most difficult days of our journey was when her blood test results came back with dangerously high potassium levels. We hadn't even realized that certain foods we thought were "healthy" could be impacting her kidneys. That day was a turning point for me—I felt a mix of fear and frustration, not knowing how I could truly help her while still allowing her to enjoy the foods she loved. I remember standing in the grocery aisle, looking at the endless labels, and feeling completely lost. It was as though every decision was critical, every ingredient could either help or harm her.

But it was that challenging moment that pushed me to dig deeper, to learn more about the foods and nutrients that would work with her kidneys rather than against them. I took that fear and turned it into a mission to not only support her but to bring joy back into our meals. Through trial and error, we found a new rhythm—simple, nourishing recipes that brought flavor and comfort back to our table. And through that process, I gained a deeper appreciation for how intentional, kidney-friendly eating can truly transform day-to-day life for people facing kidney disease.

This cookbook is my way of sharing the knowledge, recipes, and guidance I wish we'd had from the beginning. Each chapter and recipe are crafted to offer a realistic, straightforward approach to healthy eating, tailored to the needs of people with CKD—especially seniors. It's about creating a kitchen where the food is safe, delicious, and truly enjoyable. You'll find meals that are low in sodium, potassium, and phosphorus, with a focus on balanced nutrients that won't overwhelm your kidneys. We did it together, and I believe you can, too.

As you flip through these pages, remember that every small step counts. You'll be amazed at how little adjustments can lead to big changes in your health and well-being. There's no need to feel discouraged or overwhelmed. Together, we'll take it one meal at a time, creating simple, delicious dishes that support kidney health without sacrificing flavor.

So, let's dive in! Turn the page, and let's start this journey together toward eating well, living well, and making every meal count.

How to Use This Cookbook

This cookbook is more than just a collection of recipes—it's your guide to building a lifestyle that supports your kidney health. It's designed to help you take small, manageable steps toward better eating and overall wellness, with practical tools and resources tailored to your unique needs. Let me show you how to make the most of it.

How to Navigate the Book

1. **Begin with the Basics**: If you're new to managing CKD through diet and lifestyle changes, start with the first few chapters. These lay the foundation for understanding how to make kidney-friendly choices.

2. **Set Up for Success**: Use Chapter 3 to create a kidney-friendly kitchen and Chapter 4 to master meal planning and grocery shopping. These steps will make healthy eating and meal prep easier.

3. **Integrate Gentle Exercise**: Explore the exercise section to find simple movements that fit your fitness level and lifestyle. These exercises are designed to be easy on the joints and kidneys, providing benefits without overexertion.

4. **Dive Into the Recipes**: When you're ready to start cooking, turn to the recipe section. Each dish is clearly labeled to guide you on sodium, potassium, and phosphorus content, helping you choose meals that fit your specific needs.

5. **Adapt and Personalize**: Use this book as a guide, but feel free to tailor the advice and recipes to suit your preferences and circumstances. Work closely with your dietitian and healthcare team to ensure you're making the best choices for your health.

Tips for Maximizing This Book

- **Take Small Steps**: Begin with one change at a time, such as reducing salt or trying a new recipe. Small adjustments add up over time.

- **Track Your Progress**: Keep a journal of what you eat, how you feel, and any improvements you notice. This can help you stay motivated and make informed adjustments with your healthcare team.

- **Make It Enjoyable**: Experiment with the recipes, seasonings, and exercise routines. Find what works for you and brings joy to the process.

Empowering Your Journey

This book isn't about restrictions; it's about empowerment. With the right tools, knowledge, and a little patience, you can take control of your kidney health and rediscover the joys of good food and movement. Every small effort you make brings you closer to feeling stronger and healthier.

You've already taken the first step by picking up this book. Let's continue this journey together—one delicious meal and gentle stretch at a time.

Chapter 1: UNDERSTANDING KIDNEY DISEASE & NUTRITION

Anatomy of Kidney Health

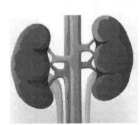

Your kidneys play an essential role in keeping your body healthy. They filter waste and excess fluids from your blood, help balance your body's minerals, and make important hormones. Healthy kidneys ensure that your blood is clean and that your body stays balanced, regulating things like blood pressure and red blood cell production.

The kidneys filter around 50 gallons of blood each day, removing waste and extra water that turn into urine. They also help maintain the proper balance of electrolytes like sodium, potassium, and calcium. When kidneys aren't working properly, waste builds up in your blood, which can cause various health issues.

This is why diet is so important. A poor diet can overwhelm your kidneys, especially if you have kidney disease. Eating the right foods helps ease the burden on your kidneys, supports their function, and may even slow the progression of kidney disease.

Progression of Chronic Kidney Disease (CKD) from Stage 3 Onwards

Chronic Kidney Disease (CKD) is a long-term condition that affects kidney function over time. Kidney disease progresses in stages, from Stage 1 (mild) to Stage 5 (end-stage kidney failure). When kidney function drops below 60%, the disease moves to Stage 3. At this stage, the kidneys are still working, but they can't filter blood as efficiently as they should.

As CKD progresses, it can lead to fluid retention, high blood pressure, and an imbalance of important minerals like potassium and phosphorus. This is why it becomes increasingly important to adjust your diet as your kidney function declines. At Stage 3 and beyond, you may need to limit foods that are high in potassium, phosphorus, and sodium, as your kidneys struggle to remove them from the blood.

Dietary changes at this stage can help prevent complications like heart disease, bone problems, and fluid overload. If kidney disease advances to Stage 4 or Stage 5, you might need dialysis or even a kidney transplant, but keeping your kidneys healthy through diet can help delay this progression.

Dietary Insights for Kidney Disease Management

Protein, Phosphorus, Potassium, and Sodium: The Essential Balancing Act

Managing your intake of four key nutrients—protein, phosphorus, potassium, and sodium—becomes crucial when you have kidney disease. These nutrients directly impact kidney function and can either ease or worsen the burden on your kidneys.

1. **Protein**: The body needs protein for growth and repair, but when the kidneys aren't functioning well, excess protein can be harmful. It can cause your kidneys to work harder to filter out waste products. If you have kidney disease, you may need to limit protein intake to reduce strain on your kidneys. However, it's important not to eliminate protein completely—your body still needs it, just in smaller amounts and from the right sources, like lean meats or plant-based proteins.

2. **Phosphorus**: Phosphorus is a mineral found in many foods, especially dairy, nuts, and processed meats. Healthy kidneys help control phosphorus levels, but when kidney function declines, phosphorus can build up in your blood, leading to weak bones and heart disease. Reducing phosphorus-rich foods and using phosphorus binders (prescribed by your doctor) may be necessary as kidney disease progresses.

3. **Potassium**: Potassium is essential for heart and muscle function. However, in kidney disease, the kidneys can't remove potassium as effectively, leading to high levels in the blood (hyperkalemia). High potassium can cause serious heart problems. Foods like bananas, oranges, and tomatoes are high in potassium, so they may need to be limited, depending on your kidney function.

4. **Sodium**: Sodium is found in salt and is used by the body to regulate fluid balance. But too much sodium can cause your body to retain excess fluid, raising blood pressure and leading to swelling. Reducing your intake of salty foods and processed items can help manage fluid balance and blood pressure, both of which are important for kidney health.

Balancing these nutrients can be tricky, but with careful meal planning and guidance from your doctor or dietitian, you can manage these key nutrients and help protect your kidneys.

Beyond Sodium: Nutrients that Impact Kidney Health You May Not Know

While sodium is a well-known nutrient to monitor in kidney disease, there are other nutrients that play a significant role in kidney health that you might not be aware of. These include:

1. **Calcium**: Too much calcium, especially when paired with high phosphorus levels, can lead to calcium deposits in the blood vessels and organs, which is harmful. You should aim to consume the right amount of calcium, mainly from food

sources like leafy greens and fortified plant milks, instead of supplements unless your doctor advises otherwise.

2. **Vitamin D**: Healthy kidneys convert vitamin D into its active form, helping your body absorb calcium. If your kidneys aren't functioning well, you may need extra vitamin D from your diet or supplements to help maintain healthy bones.

3. **Fluid**: How much fluid you need depends on the stage of kidney disease. In early stages, you may need to drink plenty of water to stay hydrated, but in later stages, fluid retention may become a problem, and you may need to limit your intake.

Being aware of these nutrients and managing them carefully can help support kidney function and prevent further damage.

Special Considerations for Seniors

For older adults, kidney disease is more common due to the natural aging process, and the body's ability to manage nutrients becomes less efficient. Seniors with kidney disease may need additional considerations, such as:

- **Elderly kidneys**: As people age, kidney function naturally declines. Seniors often have more medical conditions, like diabetes or high blood pressure, that can contribute to kidney disease. Close monitoring of kidney function and making appropriate dietary adjustments is essential.

- **Nutritional needs**: Seniors may struggle with eating enough, either due to lack of appetite or difficulties with chewing and swallowing. It's important to provide nutrient-dense foods that support kidney health without overloading the kidneys with excess protein, sodium, or phosphorus.
- **Medication interactions**: Many seniors take medications that can affect kidney function or interact with certain foods. It's important to consult your healthcare team about how your medications and diet work together.

By understanding these factors and making thoughtful dietary choices, seniors can manage their kidney health more effectively, keeping both their bodies and their kidneys strong.

The Role of Heart Health in Kidney Disease

Why a Heart-Friendly Approach is Important

The heart and kidneys are closely linked in maintaining overall health, which is why heart health plays a crucial role in managing kidney disease. Both organs are responsible for regulating fluid balance, blood pressure, and waste removal, and when one starts to fail, it can affect the other. For instance, kidney disease often leads to high blood pressure (hypertension), and conversely, heart disease can lead to kidney dysfunction.

When your kidneys aren't working properly, your body can accumulate excess fluid, causing your heart to work harder to pump blood. Over time, this added strain on the heart can lead to heart disease. In fact, people with kidney disease are at a higher risk of developing cardiovascular problems, including heart attacks and strokes. This connection is especially strong in individuals with chronic kidney disease (CKD) stages 3 to 5.

A heart-friendly approach is essential for anyone with kidney disease, as it helps reduce the risks of cardiovascular complications. By managing heart health effectively, you not only support your heart but also protect your kidneys and prevent further damage. A heart-healthy diet, combined with lifestyle changes like regular exercise, stress management, and weight control, can significantly improve both heart and kidney function.

One of the key areas of focus for heart health in kidney disease is managing cholesterol and fat levels. A diet that supports both the heart and kidneys is rich in healthy fats (like omega-3 fatty acids), low in unhealthy fats (like trans fats and saturated fats), and includes plenty of fiber, fruits, and vegetables. This balanced approach can lower cholesterol levels, prevent plaque buildup in arteries, and reduce the strain on both organs.

Managing Saturated Fat and Cholesterol: Evidence-Based Guidelines

For individuals managing kidney disease, keeping a close eye on saturated fat and cholesterol intake is crucial, as cardiovascular disease frequently accompanies kidney conditions. Saturated fats, abundant in foods such as red meat, butter, full-fat dairy products, and many processed items, are known to elevate LDL (low-density lipoprotein) cholesterol, often called "bad cholesterol." Higher LDL levels contribute to the formation of arterial plaque, heightening the risk of heart disease and stroke.

At the same time, kidney disease can make it harder to eliminate waste from the body, including excess cholesterol, which further complicates managing cholesterol levels. . To protect both your heart and kidneys, it's important to limit saturated fat intake and focus on incorporating healthier fats, such as those found in fish (like salmon and mackerel), avocados, olive oil, and nuts.

Evidence suggests that reducing saturated fat in the diet not only improves heart health but also supports kidney function. For instance, diets that are lower in saturated fats and higher in unsaturated fats are associated with a decreased risk of heart disease and kidney damage. A diet high in omega-3 fatty acids, which can be found in fatty fish and flaxseeds, has been shown to have anti-inflammatory effects that can benefit kidney health.

It's important to monitor your cholesterol intake by reducing processed foods and those high in unhealthy fats. This can prevent excessive cholesterol buildup and reduce the workload on both the heart and kidneys, promoting long-term health. Always aim for a balanced approach to fat consumption, including a variety of healthy fats to support overall heart and kidney health.

Special Diet Adjustments for Other Health Conditions

Managing Diabetes, Hypertension, and Gout in a Kidney-Friendly Diet

For individuals with kidney disease who also face diabetes, hypertension, or gout, balancing dietary needs is key to safeguarding kidney function and overall health.

1. **Diabetes**

   - Diabetes is a leading cause of kidney disease, with high blood sugar levels potentially damaging kidney blood vessels.
   - **Diet Tips:** Focus on high-fiber foods, whole grains, lean proteins, and vegetables. Avoid sugary drinks, processed snacks, and foods with added sugars to maintain stable blood sugar levels.

2. **Hypertension**

   - High blood pressure damages kidney blood vessels, impairing waste filtration.
   - **Diet Tips:** Opt for a low-sodium diet rich in fresh fruits, vegetables, whole grains, lean proteins, and low-fat dairy. Minimize processed foods and boost potassium intake with leafy greens and other kidney-friendly sources to help regulate blood pressure.

3. **Gout**

   - Gout results from excess uric acid, which can stress the kidneys and cause painful joint inflammation.
   - **Diet Tips:** Limit purine-rich foods like red meat and shellfish. Choose low-purine options such as fruits, vegetables, whole grains, and low-fat dairy. Stay well-hydrated to reduce uric acid buildup.

By tailoring your diet to manage these conditions, you can ease kidney strain and improve overall health. Consult a dietitian or healthcare provider for a personalized eating plan.

Adapting Recipes for Additional Dietary Needs

Simple modifications can make your meals kidney-friendly while addressing other health conditions:

1. **Reduce Sodium:**
   - Replace salt with herbs and spices like garlic, ginger, turmeric, or cinnamon.
   - Choose fresh or frozen vegetables over canned varieties with added salt.

2. **Adjust Protein:**
   - Use plant-based proteins (beans, lentils, tofu) or lean meats like chicken and fish.
   - Reduce overall protein intake by incorporating more vegetables and whole grains.

3. **Swap Fats:**
   - Replace butter and cream with heart-healthy fats like olive oil or avocado to support both heart and kidney health.

4. **Control Portions:**
   - Moderate servings of foods high in phosphorus, potassium, or protein to meet dietary goals without eliminating key nutrients.

By making these small adjustments, you can enjoy a variety of delicious meals while effectively managing kidney disease and coexisting conditions.

Chapter 2: THE KIDNEY-FRIENDLY DIET

Foods to Embrace For Kidney Health

Choosing the right foods became a journey for us, one that changed everything about our approach to health. When my wife was first diagnosed with kidney disease, we were overwhelmed with what felt like an endless list of dietary "do's and don'ts." But as we delved deeper, meal by meal, we learned how small, thoughtful choices could make a big difference in managing her symptoms and supporting her health. Below, I'll share the essential foods and nutrition tips that became the foundation of her kidney-friendly diet.

Proteins: Safe Sources and Serving Sizes

Protein is necessary for keeping our bodies strong and repairing cells, but in kidney disease, getting the right amount of protein is critical. When my wife began adjusting her diet, we quickly realized that too much protein could cause her kidneys to work overtime, leading to unnecessary strain. Balancing protein meant finding the right amount—not too little to stay nourished, and not too much to avoid burdening her kidneys.

We found that lean meats like chicken, turkey, and certain fish were good sources that met her needs without being overwhelming for her kidneys. When planning meals, we kept protein portions to about 3 ounces (the size of a deck of cards) and sometimes substituted with plant-based options like tofu or small portions of beans. Over time, this balance helped her body stay nourished and protected her kidneys, showing us that being mindful of protein was one of the most impactful changes we could make.

Low-Potassium Vegetables and Fruits That Still Pack Nutritional Power

Potassium is one nutrient we were cautious about since kidneys with CKD struggle to filter it effectively. We didn't want my wife's potassium levels to spike, but at the same time, she needed vegetables and fruits that would provide vitamins, fiber, and overall nutritional power. Thankfully, we found a range of options that worked well and brought color and flavor to her diet.

We leaned on **vegetables** like bell peppers, zucchini, and cauliflower, which became staples in our kitchen. These low-potassium options gave her variety and were easy to incorporate into soups, salads, and stir-fries. We learned that even leafy greens like lettuce and kale could fit into her diet in moderation, which allowed her to enjoy fresh salads without worry.

For **fruits**, apples, grapes, and berries became reliable go-tos. Berries, especially, provided her with a boost of antioxidants and were easy to enjoy fresh, in smoothies, or even as a quick snack. Apples offered fiber, which helped keep her blood sugar steady, a major advantage as managing blood sugar became part of her journey too. By choosing these low-potassium foods, we found that she could enjoy variety and nutrients without the risks associated with high-potassium produce.

Healthy Fats That Support Both Kidney and Heart Health

At first, we thought all fats would be a "no-go," but we quickly learned that healthy fats play an important role, especially with kidney and heart health often going hand in hand. Healthy fats provided my wife with energy and helped manage inflammation, which was crucial for her overall well-being.

We included foods like olive oil, avocados, and small portions of nuts (keeping in mind serving sizes to avoid excessive phosphorus). One of her favorites became a simple drizzle of olive oil over roasted vegetables or a few slices of avocado on a salad. We also added fatty fish like salmon, which brought heart-healthy omega-3s into her diet. These omega-3s proved beneficial in managing her blood pressure and reducing cholesterol, both important in CKD.

Choosing these healthy fats made a real difference. By shifting away from saturated and trans fats, her meals not only tasted rich and delicious but also contributed positively to both her heart and kidney health.

Our journey together showed us how each food choice—however small—could play a role in her overall health. Through carefully choosing safe proteins, low-potassium vegetables and fruits, and heart-friendly fats, we found a diet that not only supported her kidneys but also felt satisfying and enjoyable. With the right foods, we've turned each meal into an opportunity to boost her health, one bite at a time.

Category	Food to Embrace	Notes
Proteins	Chicken, turkey, fish (e.g., salmon), tofu, small portions of beans	Lean, kidney-friendly protein sources; keep portions around 3 ounces to avoid overloading kidneys.
Low-Potassium Vegetables	Bell peppers, zucchini, cauliflower, lettuce, kale (in moderation)	These vegetables provide essential nutrients without excessive potassium levels.
Low-Potassium Fruits	Apples, grapes, berries (e.g., strawberries, blueberries)	Antioxidant-rich fruits that help manage blood sugar and provide fiber without high potassium.
Healthy Fats	Olive oil, avocado, small portions of nuts, fatty fish (e.g., salmon)	Supports heart and kidney health; rich in omega-3s and anti-inflammatory properties.

Foods to Avoid or Limit

Choosing the right foods is essential for maintaining kidney health, but knowing which foods to avoid can be just as important. For those with chronic kidney disease (CKD), especially in the later stages, certain ingredients can put extra strain on the kidneys, making it crucial to steer clear of or limit them. As I learned through experience, helping my wife manage her diet required paying close attention not just to what was good for her, but also to the foods that could be harmful if eaten regularly.

In CKD, excess sodium, potassium, and phosphorus can overwhelm the kidneys. This section will guide you on what to watch for, and how to spot alternatives that provide nutrients without stressing your kidneys.

High-Sodium Foods to Watch Out For

Excessive sodium leads to fluid retention, swelling, and increased blood pressure, all of which can be particularly damaging for people with kidney issues. While salt may be the first thing that comes to mind, many processed foods, canned goods, and restaurant meals contain hidden sodium. Look out for foods like cured meats, frozen dinners, and salty snacks. Instead, try using herbs, spices, and sodium-free seasoning blends to enhance flavor without overloading on salt.

Potassium-Rich Foods and Alternatives

Potassium is an essential mineral, but too much of it can cause issues for those with impaired kidney function. Common high-potassium foods like bananas, oranges, and potatoes are best enjoyed sparingly or substituted with lower-potassium alternatives. For example, opting for apples or grapes instead of bananas or choosing bell peppers over tomatoes can help keep potassium intake in check while still providing variety and nutrition in meals.

Phosphorus-rich ingredients to Avoid

Phosphorus, found in dairy products, nuts, and many packaged foods, is another nutrient that can build up in the blood when kidneys aren't functioning well. High levels of phosphorus can lead to bone and heart problems, which is why it's advisable to limit or avoid certain foods. Instead of dairy milk, consider using alternatives like almond or rice milk, and choose fresh ingredients whenever possible.

Below is a helpful table listing common foods to avoid or limit to keep sodium, potassium, and phosphorus levels manageable.

Category	Foods to Avoid	Reason
High-Sodium Foods	Processed meats (e.g., bacon, sausage), canned soups, frozen dinners, snack foods (e.g., chips, pretzels)	High sodium content can lead to fluid retention and high blood pressure, stressing the kidneys.
High-Potassium Foods	Bananas, oranges, tomatoes, potatoes, avocados	These foods contain high levels of potassium that can be difficult for kidneys to process.
High-Phosphorus Foods	Dairy products (milk, cheese, yogurt), nuts, cola drinks, processed meats	High phosphorus intake can lead to bone and cardiovascular issues in CKD patients.

By keeping an eye on these ingredients and making conscious substitutions, you can maintain a kidney-friendly diet that minimizes strain on the kidneys and promotes overall health.

Navigating Common Cooking Ingredients

Navigating the world of kidney-friendly ingredients can feel overwhelming at first, but having a plan makes all the difference. When my wife and I first started managing her diet, we quickly realized that making kidney-conscious choices at the grocery store and in the kitchen wasn't just about removing certain ingredients, but also about finding the right substitutions that wouldn't compromise flavor. In this section, we'll explore how to make every ingredient in your pantry work for kidney health.

Safe Seasonings and Herbs to Replace Salt

One of the biggest changes when switching to a kidney-friendly diet is reducing sodium intake. Salt is so common in cooking that, without it, foods can feel bland. Thankfully, there are plenty of delicious alternatives that add depth and richness without straining the kidneys. Fresh or dried herbs, garlic, and spices can elevate any dish, making salt nearly unmissed.

Here's a chart of safe seasonings and herbs for a flavorful, low-sodium approach:

Seasoning	Flavor Profile	Best Used With
Garlic & Onion Powder	Savory, rich	Meats, vegetables, soups, and stews
Lemon/Lime Juice	Bright, tangy	Fish, chicken, salads, and marinades

Basil, Oregano, Thyme	Earthy, aromatic	Italian-inspired dishes, pasta, sauces
Rosemary & Sage	Woodsy, slightly piney	Roasted meats, potatoes, and veggies
Paprika & Chili Powder	Smoky, spicy	Meats, legumes, rice, and chili dishes

These seasonings not only keep meals interesting but also support a low-sodium lifestyle. Try blending different herbs and spices to create a custom seasoning mix that matches your tastes and keeps your food kidney-friendly.

How to Choose Low-Sodium, Low-Phosphorus Packaged Foods

In packaged foods, sodium and phosphorus often hide under different names or labels. Many sauces, dressings, canned goods, and frozen items have surprisingly high amounts of these additives, so it's important to read labels carefully. Here's a quick guide to help:

- **Check Sodium Levels**: Opt for products labeled as "low sodium," "reduced sodium," or "no added salt." As a general guideline, choose items that contain 140 mg of sodium or less per serving.
- **Identify Phosphorus additives**: ingredients with "phos" in their name (such as phosphate, phosphoric acid, or polyphosphates) indicate added phosphorus, which is common in processed foods and sodas. Avoid these whenever possible.

Label Reading Tips

1. **Serving Size**: Always check the serving size, as it impacts how much sodium or phosphorus you're actually consuming.
2. **% Daily Value**: Look for items with less than 5% daily value for sodium to keep intake low.
3. **Ingredient List**: If "phosphate" or similar words appear on the list, consider alternatives.

Here's an example of kidney-friendly choices when reading labels at the store:

Packaged Food	Look For	Avoid
Canned Vegetables	"No salt added" or "low sodium"	Standard canned vegetables with high salt
Soups & Broths	Low-sodium, no-salt-added versions	Regular or creamy soups with added salt
Soda & Drinks	Seltzers or unsweetened teas	Colas and dark sodas with phosphate
Dairy Alternatives	Almond or rice milk	Dairy or soy milk with added phosphorus

Reading Nutrition Labels for Kidney Health

When managing kidney health, nutrition labels become one of your best tools for making safe and healthy choices. For anyone dealing with kidney issues, understanding the specifics of sodium, potassium, and phosphorus levels on food labels is essential. Here's a simple guide to decoding these labels to ensure your food choices align with your health needs.

Understanding and Checking Sodium, Potassium, and Phosphorus on Labels

Nutrition labels provide a breakdown of macronutrients and micronutrients, including sodium, and sometimes potassium and phosphorus, though not always. Here's how to interpret these elements when they are listed:

- **Sodium**: Foods labeled as "low sodium" have 140 mg or less per serving, which is ideal for kidney health. Look at the % Daily Value (%DV) to stay below 5% per serving for sodium intake.
- **Potassium**: Potassium isn't always listed on labels, but when it is, lower potassium levels (typically below 200 mg per serving) are recommended for individuals needing to limit this mineral. Be especially cautious with canned, pre-cooked, and processed foods, which may contain hidden potassium in preservatives.
- **Phosphorus**: Like potassium, phosphorus isn't consistently shown on labels, so looking at the ingredients list is key. Avoid items with "phos" in their ingredient names, such as phosphoric acid, dipotassium phosphate, or calcium phosphate, as these are high-phosphorus additives.

Red Flags to Watch for on Packaged Foods

Many packaged foods contain added ingredients that are not ideal for kidney health. Here are some common "red flags" to watch out for:

Red Flag Ingredient	Reason to Avoid	Commonly Found In

High Sodium Content	Contributes to fluid retention, increasing blood pressure	Canned soups, sauces, frozen dinners
Added Phosphates	Quick absorption can strain kidneys	Colas, processed meats, instant foods
Potassium Chloride	High in potassium, which is often harmful for CKD	Salt substitutes, low-sodium products
Preservatives and Additives	Often high in sodium or phosphorus, leading to kidney strain	Processed foods, packaged snacks

To help simplify the label-reading process, here's a quick checklist:

- **Check Serving Size**: The listed nutrient amounts are often based on smaller servings than we usually eat. Always calculate for the portion you intend to consume.
- **Beware of Hidden** ingredients: Terms like "seasoning" or "spices" may contain added salts or phosphorus.
- **Choose "No Salt Added" or "Low Sodium" Options**: These are generally safer for kidney health. Always compare brands, as sodium content varies widely.

Using these strategies will make it easier to confidently pick kidney-friendly foods that fit into your health plan. With practice, label reading becomes second nature, ensuring that each meal supports your kidney health effectively and safely.

Chapter 3: SETTING UP YOUR KITCHEN FOR KIDNEY HEALTH

Creating a kidney-friendly kitchen is a crucial first step in managing chronic kidney disease (CKD) through diet. By transforming your kitchen into a space that fosters healthier eating habits, you're not just setting yourself up for success in managing your condition; you're also laying the foundation for a sustainable, long-term approach to better health. Let's walk you through the key elements to consider when setting up your kitchen for kidney health.

Organizing Your Pantry

Your pantry is the heart of your kitchen, where many of your kidney-friendly foods will be stored. Begin by removing foods that may be high in sodium, potassium, and phosphorus, as well as packaged or processed foods that are typically high in unhealthy fats or added sugars. Focus on organizing your pantry with kidney-healthy staples like:

- **Unsweetened nut butters** or seeds for snacks or spreads
- **Olive Oil**: A heart-healthy fat that is low in saturated fat and high in monounsaturated fats, ideal for cooking or drizzling on vegetables.
- **Herbs and Spices**: Garlic, basil, oregano, turmeric, rosemary, and thyme are great ways to enhance

flavor without adding salt. You can also use salt-free seasoning blends to add variety.

- **Low-Sodium Broth**: Keep low-sodium vegetable, chicken, or beef broth on hand for soups, stews, or gravies. This helps you control your sodium intake while still adding depth of flavor.

- **Whole Grains**: Brown rice, quinoa, and whole wheat pasta are all kidney-friendly grains that provide fiber without overloading the kidneys with phosphorus. They also serve as great bases for many meals.

- **Canned or Frozen Vegetables (Low-Sodium)**: Keep a stash of low-sodium canned vegetables or frozen veggies like green beans, peas, and cauliflower for when fresh produce isn't available.

- **Legumes and Lentils**: Beans, lentils, and chickpeas are excellent plant-based protein sources. If you are in the early stages of kidney disease, these can be a great addition to your diet in moderate portions.

It's important to make sure the foods you store are ones that support kidney health. You may even want to label shelves for easy access to low-sodium options or low-potassium vegetables. Think of your pantry as your tool for healthy living – everything in it should support your kidney journey.

Smart Refrigerator Setup

The fridge is where your fresh foods should be stored, and how you organize it will make a big difference in maintaining a kidney-friendly diet. For CKD, you'll want to keep a variety of fresh, low-potassium fruits and vegetables on hand, along with lean protein options like chicken or fish.

Consider these tips:

- **Fresh fruits and vegetables**: Keep your fridge stocked with kidney-friendly options like berries, apples, cauliflower, and bell peppers. Prepare them in easy-to-use portions so they are ready for cooking or snacking.

- **Lean proteins**: If you're choosing to eat animal proteins, be sure to store lean cuts of meat, like skinless chicken breast, turkey, and fresh fish such as salmon or tilapia. For vegetarians, tofu, tempeh, and legumes (again, low-sodium) are great options.

- **Pre-cut and prepped veggies**: Spend a little time each week prepping your vegetables so that they are ready to use. Having them washed, peeled, and cut helps save time and makes it easier to prepare meals quickly.

A well-organized fridge ensures you can quickly access kidney-friendly ingredients, helping you stick to your healthy eating plan.

Your Kidney-Friendly Cooking Tools

Investing in the right kitchen tools can make cooking kidney-friendly meals much easier and enjoyable. Here's a list of tools that are helpful for kidney health:

- **Sharp Knives**: A good set of knives makes meal prep easier and faster, reducing the time spent chopping and slicing vegetables and proteins.
- **Cutting Board**: Choose a sturdy, spacious cutting board that is easy to clean. To avoid cross-contamination, consider using separate boards for meat and vegetables.
- **Slow Cooker/Pressure Cooker/Air fryer**: These appliances are great for cooking lean meats, beans, and vegetables without requiring much added salt. You can make large batches of kidney-friendly meals to last throughout the week.
- **Non-stick pans**: They help you cook with less oil, reducing the overall fat content in your meals while preventing sticking.
- **Food processor**: A food processor helps in prepping large amounts of vegetables, making chopping and dicing more efficient.
- **Blender**: Use a blender to make healthy smoothies with kidney-friendly fruits, or even to puree soups and stews that can be high in nutritional value.
- **Measuring cups and spoons**: These ensure that your portions are correct, especially when it comes to sensitive ingredients like protein or phosphorus.
- **Steamer**: Steaming is an excellent way to prepare vegetables without added fats or salt. It locks in nutrients, ensuring that you retain the most vitamins and minerals.
- **Roasting pans**: Roasting your vegetables and lean proteins is a healthy alternative to frying. A good roasting pan can help evenly cook food while maintaining its flavor.

- **Grill pan**: Grilling is a great way to cook without adding unnecessary fats. Use a grill pan to get that smoky flavor without going overboard with oil or salt.

These tools promote healthy cooking methods, reducing the need for processed ingredients that may contain excess salt, phosphorus, or unhealthy fats.

Labeling & Storage

Organizing and labeling your kitchen can make following a kidney-friendly diet much easier. Use labeled storage boxes or bags to clearly mark kidney-friendly items in your pantry and fridge. Keep low-sodium, low-potassium options at the front for easy access, ensuring healthier choices are always within reach.

Creating a kidney-friendly kitchen isn't just about removing unhealthy foods—it's about building an environment that encourages fresh, nutritious, and kidney-supportive meals. By staying organized, stocking your kitchen with the right ingredients, using helpful tools, and shopping smart, you set yourself up for success.

When I first started helping my wife manage her kidney disease through diet, our kitchen became the cornerstone of her health journey. With time and effort, we transformed our habits, and the results were worth it—she felt stronger, more energized, and in control. Healthy eating became more than a requirement; it became a way to embrace life. With a thoughtfully organized kitchen, you too can make meaningful changes and enjoy the benefits of a kidney-friendly diet.

Chapter 4: BREAKFASTS TO START THE DAY RIGHT

Berry Bliss Smoothie

Preparation Time: 5 minutes | **Serving Size:** 1 serving

INGREDIENTS

- 1/2 cup fresh or frozen blueberries (low-potassium)
- 1/2 cup fresh or frozen strawberries, hulled
- 1/4 cup unsweetened almond milk (or kidney-friendly milk alternative)
- 1/4 cup water
- 1 tbsp chia seeds (optional, for added fiber)
- 1/2 tsp vanilla extract
- Ice cubes (optional, for desired thickness)

INSTRUCTIONS

1. **place all ingredients** in a blender.
2. Blend on high until smooth and creamy, adjusting the amount of water for desired consistency.
3. Pour into a glass, add ice cubes if desired, and enjoy immediately.

TIPS & MODIFICATIONS

For a Thicker Smoothie: Add a few more chia seeds and let the smoothie sit for 5 minutes to thicken.

Storage: Smoothie is best enjoyed fresh but can be refrigerated for up to 12 hours in a sealed jar.

Optional Boosts: Add a small handful of spinach for extra fiber and antioxidants without significantly increasing potassium levels.

NUTRITIONAL BREAKDOWN (APPROXIMATE)
Protein: 3g | Potassium: 150mg | Sodium: 40mg | Fiber: 6g | Healthy Fats: 2g

Tropical Sunrise Smoothie

Preparation Time: 5 minutes | **Serving Size:** 1 serving

INGREDIENTS
- 1/2 cup fresh or frozen pineapple chunks
- 1/4 cup unsweetened coconut milk
- 1/4 cup water
- 1 tbsp ground flaxseeds (optional, for extra fiber)
- 1 tsp fresh lime juice
- Ice cubes (optional, for a cooler drink)

INSTRUCTIONS
1. Combine all ingredients in a blender.
2. Blend on high until smooth and creamy, adding more water if needed for a thinner consistency.
3. Pour into a glass, garnish with a slice of lime, and enjoy.

TIPS & MODIFICATIONS
- **For Added Sweetness:** Add a few slices of fresh mango (mindful of potassium content) if tolerated.
- **Storage:** Best enjoyed fresh but can be stored in the fridge for up to 12 hours.

NUTRITIONAL BREAKDOWN (APPROXIMATE)
Protein: 2g | Potassium: 120mg | Sodium: 25mg | Fiber: 4g | Healthy Fats: 3g

Green Goodness Smoothie

Preparation Time: 5 minutes | **Serving Size:** 1 serving

INGREDIENTS
- 1/2 cup baby spinach (low-potassium greens)
- 1/4 cup cucumber, chopped
- 1/4 cup frozen pineapple chunks
- 1/4 cup unsweetened almond milk
- 1/4 cup water
- 1/2 tsp fresh lemon juice

INSTRUCTIONS
1. Add all ingredients to a blender.
2. Blend until smooth, adding water as needed to reach your desired consistency.
3. Pour into a glass and enjoy the fresh, detoxifying taste.

TIPS & MODIFICATIONS
Add Fiber: Sprinkle in 1 tsp chia seeds for added fiber, but let the smoothie sit for a few minutes to thicken.
Storage: Drink immediately for best taste and nutrient retention.

NUTRITIONAL BREAKDOWN (APPROXIMATE)
Protein: 2g | Potassium: 160mg | Sodium: 20mg | Fiber: 3g | Healthy Fats: 1g

Apple Cinnamon Delight Smoothie

Preparation Time: 5 minutes | **Serving Size:** 1 serving

INGREDIENTS
- 1/2 medium apple, cored and chopped (leave the peel on for fiber)
- 1/4 cup unsweetened almond milk
- 1/4 cup water
- 1/2 tsp ground cinnamon
- 1 tbsp chia seeds (for added fiber)
- Ice cubes (optional, for thickness)

INSTRUCTIONS
1. Add all **INGREDIENTS** to a blender.
2. Blend until smooth, adding more water for a thinner consistency.
3. Pour into a glass, sprinkle with a dash of cinnamon if desired, and enjoy.

TIPS & MODIFICATIONS
Sweeten Naturally: Add a few pieces of ripe pear if you prefer a slightly sweeter smoothie.
Storage: Store in the fridge for up to 12 hours if needed but best enjoyed fresh.

NUTRITIONAL BREAKDOWN (APPROXIMATE)
Protein: 3g | *Potassium:* 140mg | *Sodium:* 15mg | *Fiber:* 5g | *Healthy Fats:* 2g

Strawberry Almond Dream Smoothie

Preparation Time: 5 minutes | ***Serving Size:*** 1 serving

INGREDIENTS
- 1/2 cup fresh or frozen strawberries
- 1/4 cup unsweetened almond milk
- 1/4 cup water
- 1 tbsp ground flaxseed (for added fiber and healthy fats)
- 1/2 tsp vanilla extract
- Ice cubes (optional)

INSTRUCTIONS
1. Add all ingredients to a blender.
2. Blend on high until smooth and creamy.
3. Pour into a glass, add ice if desired, and enjoy a refreshing, creamy smoothie.

TIPS & MODIFICATIONS

Thicken It Up: For a thicker consistency, add 1-2 tbsp of chia seeds and let sit for a few minutes.

Storage: Best enjoyed fresh; if needed, refrigerate up to 12 hours.

NUTRITIONAL BREAKDOWN (APPROXIMATE)
Protein: 3g | *Potassium:* 130mg | *Sodium:* 15mg | *Fiber:* 4g | *Healthy Fats:* 3g

Heart-Healthy Oatmeal

Cooking Time: 5 minutes | ***Preparation Time:*** 5 minutes | ***Serving Size:*** 1 bowl

INGREDIENTS
- 1/2 cup rolled oats (quick-cooking)
- 1 cup water or unsweetened almond milk
- 1/2 tbsp chia seeds
- 1/2 tbsp ground flaxseed
- 1/4 tsp ground cinnamon
- 1/4 cup fresh berries (such as strawberries or blueberries)

INSTRUCTIONS

1. In a small saucepan, bring water or almond milk to a boil.
2. Add oats, chia seeds, flaxseed, and cinnamon. Reduce heat and simmer for about 5 minutes, stirring occasionally until creamy.
3. Transfer to a bowl, top with fresh berries, and enjoy.

TIPS & MODIFICATIONS

For Extra Creaminess: Use unsweetened coconut or almond milk instead of water.

Storage: Can be refrigerated for up to 2 days and reheated with a splash of water or milk.

NUTRITIONAL BREAKDOWN (APPROXIMATE)

Protein: 6g | Potassium: 110mg | Sodium: 10mg | Fiber: 7g | Healthy Fats: 4g

Cinnamon Apple Quinoa Porridge

Cooking Time: 15 minutes | **Preparation Time:** 5 minutes | **Serving Size:** 1 bowl

INGREDIENTS

- 1/4 cup quinoa, rinsed
- 3/4 cup water
- 1/4 medium apple, chopped
- 1/2 tsp ground cinnamon
- 1/2 tsp vanilla extract (optional)
- 1 tsp maple syrup or honey (optional)

INSTRUCTIONS

1. In a small pot, bring quinoa and water to a boil.
2. Reduce heat, cover, and simmer for about 12 minutes or until quinoa is tender and water is absorbed.
3. Stir in chopped apple and cinnamon, simmering for an additional 3 minutes.
4. Serve in a bowl, adding vanilla extract or maple syrup if desired.

TIPS & MODIFICATIONS
Texture Preference: Adjust cooking time for softer or firmer quinoa.

Storage: Store in the fridge for up to 3 days and reheat as needed.

NUTRITIONAL BREAKDOWN (APPROXIMATE)
Protein: 4g | Potassium: 95mg | Sodium: 5mg | Fiber: 5g | Healthy Fats: 1g

Chia Flax Fiber Porridge

Preparation Time: 5 minutes + overnight soaking | **Serving Size:** 1 bowl

INGREDIENTS
- 1 tbsp chia seeds
- 1 tbsp ground flaxseed
- 1/2 cup unsweetened almond milk
- 1/4 tsp ground cinnamon
- 1/4 cup fresh berries (optional)

INSTRUCTIONS
1. In a small bowl, combine chia seeds, flaxseed, almond milk, and cinnamon.
2. Stir well, cover, and refrigerate overnight.
3. In the morning, stir and top with fresh berries if desired.

TIPS & MODIFICATIONS
Thicker Texture: Add 1/4 cup additional almond milk if needed.
Storage: Keeps in the fridge for up to 2 days.

NUTRITIONAL BREAKDOWN (APPROXIMATE)
Protein: 5g | Potassium: 85mg | Sodium: 15mg | Fiber: 8g | Healthy Fats: 6g

Coconut Oats Delight

Cooking Time: 5 minutes | **Preparation Time:** 5 minutes | **Serving Size:** 1 bowl

INGREDIENTS
- 1/2 cup rolled oats
- 1/2 cup unsweetened coconut milk
- 1/2 cup water
- 1/4 cup chopped strawberries or blueberries
- 1 tsp unsweetened shredded coconut (optional)

INSTRUCTIONS
1. In a small pot, bring coconut milk and water to a simmer.
2. Stir in oats and cook for 5 minutes, stirring frequently.
3. Serve topped with strawberries and shredded coconut.

TIPS & MODIFICATIONS
Flavor Variation: Add 1/4 tsp vanilla extract.
Storage: Refrigerate for up to 2 days, adding a splash of milk when reheating.

NUTRITIONAL BREAKDOWN (APPROXIMATE)
Protein: 5g | Potassium: 90mg | Sodium: 8mg | Fiber: 6g | Healthy Fats: 4g

Pumpkin Spice Oatmeal

Cooking Time: 5 minutes | **Preparation Time:** 5 minutes | **Serving Size:** 1 bowl

INGREDIENTS
- 1/2 cup rolled oats
- 1 cup water or unsweetened almond milk
- 2 tbsp pumpkin puree (no added sugar)
- 1/2 tsp ground cinnamon
- 1/4 tsp ground nutmeg (optional)

INSTRUCTIONS
1. In a small pot, bring water or almond milk to a boil.
2. Add oats and reduce heat, cooking for 5 minutes.
3. Stir in pumpkin puree, cinnamon, and nutmeg, then serve warm.

TIPS & MODIFICATIONS

Additional Toppings: Add a sprinkle of chia seeds for more fiber.

Storage: Can be refrigerated for up to 2 days; add more liquid when reheating.

NUTRITIONAL BREAKDOWN (APPROXIMATE)
Protein: 6g | Potassium: 120mg | Sodium: 10mg | Fiber: 5g | Healthy Fats: 2g

Savory Veggie Rice Bowl

Cooking Time: 10 minutes | **Preparation Time:** 5 minutes | **Serving Size:** 1 bowl

INGREDIENTS
- 1/2 cup cooked brown rice
- 1/4 cup chopped bell peppers (red or yellow)
- 1/4 cup cucumber, diced
- 1 tbsp fresh parsley or basil, chopped
- 1 tsp extra-virgin olive oil
- Freshly ground black pepper to taste

INSTRUCTIONS
1. Prepare the brown rice according to package instructions, omitting any salt.
2. In a bowl, combine cooked rice, bell peppers, cucumber, and fresh herbs.
3. Drizzle with olive oil and season with black pepper.
4. Toss gently and enjoy.

TIPS & MODIFICATIONS

Add Extra Crunch: Top with a few unsalted sunflower seeds.

Storage: Store in the fridge for up to 1 day.

NUTRITIONAL BREAKDOWN (APPROXIMATE)
Protein: 4g | Potassium: 120mg | Sodium: 5mg | Fiber: 3g | Healthy Fats: 5g

Quinoa Avocado Power Bowl

Cooking Time: 15 minutes | **Prep. Time:** 5 minutes | **Serving Size:** 1 bowl

INGREDIENTS
- 1/2 cup cooked quinoa
- 1/4 avocado, sliced
- 5 cherry tomatoes, halved
- 1/2 tsp lemon juice
- 1 tsp extra-virgin olive oil
- Fresh herbs like basil or cilantro, chopped

INSTRUCTIONS
1. Cook quinoa according to package instructions, without adding salt.
2. In a bowl, combine quinoa, sliced avocado, and cherry tomatoes.
3. Drizzle with lemon juice and olive oil, and garnish with fresh herbs.
4. Gently mix and serve.

TIPS & MODIFICATIONS
For Extra Flavor: Add a pinch of paprika or ground black pepper.
Storage: Best enjoyed fresh due to the avocado.

NUTRITIONAL BREAKDOWN (APPROXIMATE)
Protein: 6g | Potassium: 150mg | Sodium: 10mg | Fiber: 5g | Healthy Fats: 7g

Sweet Potato and Spinach Breakfast Bowl

Cooking Time: 20 minutes | **Preparation Time:** 5 minutes | **Serving Size:** 1 bowl

INGREDIENTS
- 1/2 small sweet potato, peeled and cubed
- 1 cup fresh spinach
- 1 tsp olive oil
- Fresh ground black pepper to taste

INSTRUCTIONS
1. Preheat oven to 375°F (190°C). Toss sweet potato cubes in 1/2 tsp olive oil and roast for 15 minutes, until tender.
2. In a skillet, heat the remaining olive oil and

sauté spinach for 2-3 minutes, until wilted.
3. In a bowl, combine roasted sweet potatoes and spinach, seasoning with black pepper.
4. Serve warm.

TIPS & MODIFICATIONS

For Extra Texture: Top with a sprinkle of sesame seeds.
Storage: Store in the fridge for up to 1 day.

NUTRITIONAL BREAKDOWN (APPROXIMATE)
Protein: 3g | *Potassium:* 180mg | *Sodium:* 8mg | *Fiber:* 4g | *Healthy Fats:* 4g

Zucchini Noodle Bowl

Cooking Time: 5 minutes | **Preparation Time:** 5 minutes | **Serving Size:** 1 bowl

INGREDIENTS
- 1/2 zucchini, spiralized into noodles
- 2 egg whites
- 1/4 avocado, sliced
- Fresh herbs like basil or parsley, chopped
- 1 tsp olive oil

INSTRUCTIONS
1. Heat olive oil in a skillet over medium heat and sauté zucchini noodles for 1-2 minutes until slightly tender.
2. In the same skillet, scramble egg whites until cooked through.
3. In a bowl, combine zucchini noodles and scrambled egg whites. Top with avocado slices and fresh herbs.
4. Serve warm.

TIPS & MODIFICATIONS
- **Alternative Flavor:** Add a pinch of black pepper or red pepper flakes.
- **Storage:** Best enjoyed fresh.

NUTRITIONAL BREAKDOWN (APPROXIMATE)
Protein: 8g | Potassium: 90mg | Sodium: 5mg | Fiber: 3g | Healthy Fats: 6g

Berry Breakfast Quinoa Bowl

Cooking Time: 15 minutes | **Preparation Time:** 5 minutes | **Serving Size:** 1 bowl

INGREDIENTS
- 1/2 cup cooked quinoa
- 1/4 cup mixed berries (e.g., strawberries, blueberries)
- 1/2 tsp honey (optional)
- 1/4 tsp ground cinnamon

INSTRUCTIONS
1. Prepare quinoa as per package instructions, omitting salt.
2. In a bowl, combine quinoa, mixed berries, and cinnamon.
3. Drizzle with honey if desired.
4. Gently mix and serve.

TIPS & MODIFICATIONS
Additional Toppings: Add a few unsweetened coconut flakes for texture.
Storage: Can be refrigerated for up to 1 day.

NUTRITIONAL BREAKDOWN (APPROXIMATE)
Protein: 5g | Potassium: 95mg | Sodium: 8mg | Fiber: 4g | Healthy Fats: 2g

Egg White Scramble with Spinach and Tomatoes

Cooking Time: 5 minutes | **Preparation Time:** 5 minutes | **Serving Size:** 1 serving

INGREDIENTS
- 3 large egg whites
- 1/4 cup fresh spinach, chopped
- 1/4 cup cherry tomatoes, halved
- 1 tsp olive oil
- Freshly ground black pepper, to taste

INSTRUCTIONS
1. In a nonstick skillet, heat olive oil over medium heat.
2. Add the spinach and tomatoes, and cook for 1-2 minutes until slightly softened.

3. Add egg whites to the skillet and gently scramble, cooking until they are set but still soft.
4. Season with black pepper and serve warm.

TIPS & MODIFICATIONS

Flavor Boost: Add a sprinkle of fresh herbs like parsley or chives.

Storage: Best enjoyed immediately but can be refrigerated for up to 1 day.

NUTRITIONAL BREAKDOWN (APPROXIMATE)
Protein: 10g | Potassium: 100mg | Sodium: 55mg | Fiber: 1g | Healthy Fats: 3g

Tofu Scramble with Bell Peppers

Cooking Time: 5 minutes | **Preparation Time:** 5 minutes | **Serving Size:** 1 serving

INGREDIENTS
- 1/4 cup firm tofu, crumbled
- 1/4 cup red bell pepper, diced
- 1/4 cup yellow bell pepper, diced
- 1 tsp olive oil
- 1/8 tsp turmeric (optional, for color)
- Freshly ground black pepper, to taste

INSTRUCTIONS
1. Heat olive oil in a skillet over medium heat.
2. Add bell peppers and cook for 2-3 minutes until they begin to soften.
3. Add crumbled tofu and turmeric, stirring gently until everything is warm and combined.
4. Season with black pepper and serve immediately.

TIPS & MODIFICATIONS

Extra Flavor: Add fresh herbs like basil or parsley.

Storage: Can be refrigerated for up to 2 days.

NUTRITIONAL BREAKDOWN (APPROXIMATE)
Protein: 6g | Potassium: 90mg | Sodium: 20mg | Fiber: 2g | Healthy Fats: 3g

Egg White Veggie Omelette

Cooking Time: 7 minutes | **Preparation Time:** 5 minutes | **Serving Size:** 1 serving

INGREDIENTS
- 3 large egg whites
- 1/4 cup diced bell pepper
- 1/4 cup diced zucchini
- 1 tsp olive oil
- Fresh parsley, chopped, for garnish
- Freshly ground black pepper, to taste

INSTRUCTIONS
1. In a nonstick skillet, heat olive oil over medium heat.
2. Add bell pepper and zucchini, and cook for 2-3 minutes until soft.
3. Pour egg whites over the veggies, swirling to coat the pan.
4. Allow to cook undisturbed until set, then fold in half.
5. Garnish with parsley and season with black pepper before serving.

TIPS & MODIFICATIONS
Additional Flavor: Add a pinch of paprika or smoked paprika for an extra kick.
Storage: Best enjoyed fresh.

NUTRITIONAL BREAKDOWN (APPROXIMATE)
Protein: 10g | Potassium: 85mg | Sodium: 60mg | Fiber: 2g | Healthy Fats: 4g

Poached Eggs on Whole Wheat Toast

Cooking Time: 5 minutes | **Preparation Time:** 5 minutes | **Serving Size:** 1 serving

INGREDIENTS
- 2 large egg whites
- 1 slice whole wheat bread
- Fresh parsley or chives, chopped, for garnish
- Freshly ground black pepper, to taste

INSTRUCTIONS
1. Bring a small pot of water to a gentle simmer.

2. Carefully slide egg whites into the water, cooking for 2-3 minutes until set.
3. Toast whole wheat bread, then top with poached egg whites.
4. Garnish with fresh herbs and black pepper before serving.

TIPS & MODIFICATIONS
For Extra Flavor: Add a dash of balsamic vinegar or a squeeze of lemon juice.
Storage: Best enjoyed immediately.

NUTRITIONAL BREAKDOWN (APPROXIMATE)
Protein: 8g | Potassium: 70mg | Sodium: 65mg | Fiber: 3g | Healthy Fats: 0.5g

Egg White and Avocado Breakfast Wrap

Cooking Time: 5 minutes | **Preparation Time:** 5 minutes | **Serving Size:** 1 wrap

INGREDIENTS
- 2 large egg whites
- 1/4 avocado, sliced
- 1/4 cup fresh spinach, chopped
- 1 small whole wheat tortilla
- Freshly ground black pepper, to taste

INSTRUCTIONS
1. In a nonstick skillet, scramble egg whites over medium heat until cooked through.
2. Warm the tortilla in a pan or microwave, then layer with spinach, scrambled egg whites, and avocado slices.
3. Season with black pepper, roll up the wrap, and serve.

TIPS & MODIFICATIONS
Make It Spicy: Add a dash of black pepper or a few crushed red pepper flakes.
Storage: Can be wrapped and stored in the fridge for up to 1 day.

NUTRITIONAL BREAKDOWN (APPROXIMATE)
Protein: 9g | Potassium: 150mg | Sodium: 70mg | Fiber: 5g | Healthy Fats: 6g

Berry Quinoa Breakfast Bowl

***Cooking Time**: 15 minutes | **Preparation Time**: 5 minutes | **Serving Size**: 1 bowl*

INGREDIENT LIST:
- 1/2 cup quinoa (cooked)
- 1/4 cup fresh blueberries
- 1/4 cup fresh strawberries, sliced
- 1 tbsp chia seeds
- 1 tsp honey (optional)
- 1/4 cup unsweetened almond milk

INSTRUCTIONS:
1. Cook quinoa according to package instructions, using water or low-sodium vegetable broth for added flavor.
2. In a bowl, combine cooked quinoa with fresh berries.
3. Drizzle almond milk over the top and add chia seeds.
4. If desired, drizzle a small amount of honey for extra sweetness.
5. Gently stir and enjoy as a light, energizing breakfast.

TIPS & MODIFICATIONS:
Swap the berries for other low-potassium fruits like pears or apples if preferred. For a nutty twist, top with a handful of unsalted almonds or walnuts.

NUTRITIONAL BREAKDOWN:
Sugar: 12g | Fiber: 5g | Potassium: 150mg | Sodium: 5mg

Avocado and Egg Breakfast Wrap

***Cooking Time**: 10 minutes | **Preparation Time**: 5 minutes | **Serving Size**: 1 wrap*

INGREDIENT LIST:
- 2 large eggs
- 1/2 avocado, mashed
- 1 small whole wheat tortilla (low-sodium)
- 1 tbsp fresh cilantro or parsley (optional)
- 1 tsp olive oil
- Freshly ground black pepper, to taste

INSTRUCTIONS:
1. In a skillet, heat olive oil over medium heat.

2. Crack the eggs into the skillet and scramble until fully cooked.
3. Warm the tortilla in the same skillet for 1-2 minutes.
4. Spread mashed avocado onto the tortilla.
5. Add scrambled eggs and fresh cilantro or parsley.
6. Season with black pepper, fold the wrap, and enjoy a filling breakfast.

TIPS & MODIFICATIONS:
Add fresh spinach or kale for extra nutrients without adding too much potassium. Try swapping the whole wheat tortilla for a low-sodium, gluten-free option.

NUTRITIONAL BREAKDOWN:
Sugar: 1g | *Fiber*: 7g | *Potassium*: 350mg | *Sodium*: 150mg

Oatmeal with Apples and Cinnamon

Cooking Time: 10 minutes | **Preparation Time**: 5 minutes | **Serving Size**: 1 bowl

INGREDIENT LIST:
- 1/2 cup rolled oats
- 1/2 apple, diced
- 1/2 tsp cinnamon
- 1 tsp agave syrup
- 1/4 cup unsweetened almond milk
- 1/4 cup water

INSTRUCTIONS:
1. In a small pot, bring the water and almond milk to a boil.
2. Add oats and reduce heat to low. Cook for about 5-7 minutes, stirring occasionally.
3. Stir in diced apple and cinnamon once the oats are soft.
4. Drizzle with agave syrup for sweetness and serve hot.

TIPS & MODIFICATIONS:
For a dairy-free option, use coconut milk instead of almond milk. Add a sprinkle of chia seeds for extra fiber.

NUTRITIONAL BREAKDOWN:
Sugar: 10g | Fiber: 4g | Potassium: 130mg | Sodium: 2mg

Coconut Almond Chia Pudding

Cooking Time: 5 minutes (no cooking required) | **Preparation Time**: 5 minutes | **Serving Size**: 1 serving

INGREDIENT LIST:
- 2 tbsp chia seeds
- 1/2 cup unsweetened coconut milk
- 1 tbsp almond butter
- 1/2 tsp vanilla extract
- 1 tbsp slivered almonds (for topping)

INSTRUCTIONS:
1. In a jar or bowl, mix chia seeds, coconut milk, almond butter, and vanilla extract.
2. Stir well and refrigerate for at least 2 hours or overnight for the pudding to thicken.
3. Once thickened, top with slivered almonds and enjoy.

TIPS & MODIFICATIONS:
Use a different nut butter like cashew or peanut butter if desired.
For a sweeter version, add a little honey or maple syrup.

NUTRITIONAL BREAKDOWN:
Sugar: 2g | Fiber: 10g | Potassium: 160mg | Sodium: 15mg

Peach and Yogurt Parfait

Cooking Time: 5 minutes | **Preparation Time**: 5 minutes | **Serving Size**: 1 serving

INGREDIENT LIST:
- 1/2 cup plain Greek yogurt (low-sodium)
- 1/2 peach, sliced
- 1 tsp cinnamon
- 1 tbsp granola (low-sodium, optional)

INSTRUCTIONS:
1. In a glass or bowl, layer Greek yogurt and sliced peaches.
2. Sprinkle cinnamon on top for extra flavor.
3. Add a handful of granola for a crunchy texture if desired.

4. Serve immediately or refrigerate for a quick grab-and-go option.

TIPS & MODIFICATIONS:
Substitute peaches with other low-potassium fruits like berries or pears.
For extra crunch, add chia seeds or sliced almonds instead of granola.

NUTRITIONAL BREAKDOWN:
Sugar: 8g | Fiber: 3g | Potassium: 250mg | Sodium: 50mg

Low-Sodium Sweet Potato Hash

Cooking Time: 15 minutes | **Preparation Time**: 10 minutes | **Serving Size**: 1 serving

INGREDIENT LIST:
- 1 medium sweet potato, peeled and diced
- 1/4 cup red bell pepper, diced
- 1/4 cup yellow onion, diced
- 1 tsp olive oil
- 2 egg whites
- Fresh herbs (optional)

INSTRUCTIONS:
1. In a skillet, heat olive oil over medium heat.
2. Add diced sweet potatoes and cook for about 8-10 minutes until tender.
3. Add red bell pepper and onion to the skillet and sauté until softened.
4. In a separate pan, scramble egg whites and set aside.
5. Serve the sweet potato hash with scrambled egg whites on the side or mixed in for extra protein.

TIPS & MODIFICATIONS:
For added flavor, sprinkle with a pinch of cinnamon or paprika. You can also use other vegetables like zucchini or spinach for variety.

NUTRITIONAL BREAKDOWN:
Sugar: 5g | Fiber: 4g | Potassium: 250mg | Sodium: 10mg

Chapter 5: ENERGIZING LUNCHES

Crisp Cucumber & Herb Salad with Lemon Vinaigrette

Preparation Time: 10 minutes | **Serving Size:** 2

INGREDIENTS:
- 1 large cucumber, thinly sliced
- 1/4 cup fresh parsley, chopped
- 1/4 cup fresh dill, chopped
- 1/4 cup fresh mint leaves, chopped
- 2 tablespoons extra virgin olive oil
- 1 tablespoon fresh lemon juice
- 1/2 teaspoon lemon zest
- Freshly ground black pepper, to taste

INSTRUCTIONS:
1. In a large salad bowl, combine the cucumber slices, parsley, dill, and mint.
2. In a small bowl, whisk together olive oil, lemon juice, lemon zest, and black pepper.
3. Drizzle the lemon vinaigrette over the salad, tossing gently to combine.
4. Serve immediately or chill in the refrigerator for 10 minutes for added flavor.

TIPS & MODIFICATIONS:
For added crunch, toss in a few thinly sliced radishes. To maintain freshness, store in an airtight container in the refrigerator for up to 24 hours.

Nutritional Breakdown (per serving):
Protein: 1g, Potassium: 120 mg, Sodium: 5 mg, Fiber: 2g, Healthy Fats: 10g

Colorful Quinoa & Veggie Medley

Cooking Time: 15 minutes | **Preparation Time:** 10 minutes | **Serving Size:** 2

INGREDIENTS:
- 1/2 cup cooked quinoa
- 1/4 cup red bell pepper, diced
- 1/4 cup yellow bell pepper, diced
- 1/4 cup cucumber, diced
- 1/4 cup fresh parsley, chopped
- 1 tablespoon olive oil
- 1 tablespoon apple cider vinegar
- Freshly ground black pepper, to taste

INSTRUCTIONS:
1. In a medium salad bowl, combine the cooked quinoa, bell peppers, cucumber, and parsley.
2. In a small bowl, whisk together olive oil, apple cider vinegar, and black pepper.
3. Pour the dressing over the quinoa and vegetables, tossing to coat evenly.
4. Serve chilled or at room temperature.

TIPS & MODIFICATIONS:
For a change in texture, substitute quinoa with millet. You can store the dish in the refrigerator for up to 2 days in an airtight container.

Nutritional Breakdown (per serving):
Protein: 4g, Potassium: 150 mg, Sodium: 6 mg, Fiber: 3g, Healthy Fats: 7g

Berry & Spinach Salad with Poppy Seed Dressing

Preparation Time: 10 minutes | **Serving Size:** 2

INGREDIENTS:
- 2 cups baby spinach
- 1/2 cup fresh strawberries, sliced
- 1/2 cup fresh blueberries
- 1/4 cup feta cheese (optional, low-sodium)

- 1 tablespoon extra virgin olive oil
- 1 teaspoon apple cider vinegar
- 1/2 teaspoon poppy seeds
- Freshly ground black pepper, to taste

INSTRUCTIONS:
1. In a salad bowl, layer the baby spinach, strawberries, and blueberries. Sprinkle with feta if using.
2. In a small bowl, whisk together olive oil, apple cider vinegar, poppy seeds, and black pepper.
3. Drizzle the poppy seed dressing over the salad and toss gently.
4. Serve immediately for the best flavor.

TIPS & MODIFICATIONS:
For a nutty crunch, add a few sliced almonds. Store without dressing for up to a day in the refrigerator.

Nutritional Breakdown (per serving):
Protein: 2g, Potassium: 160 mg, Sodium: 10 mg, Fiber: 3g, Healthy Fats: 8g

Low-Potassium Greek Chickpea Salad

Preparation Time: 10 minutes | **Serving Size:** 2

INGREDIENTS:
- 1/2 cup canned chickpeas, rinsed and drained
- 1/4 cup cucumber, diced
- 1/4 cup red bell pepper, diced
- 1/4 cup cherry tomatoes, halved
- 2 tablespoons fresh parsley, chopped
- 1 tablespoon extra virgin olive oil
- 1 tablespoon lemon juice
- Freshly ground black pepper, to taste

INSTRUCTIONS:
1. In a salad bowl, combine the chickpeas, cucumber, bell pepper, tomatoes, and parsley.
2. In a small bowl, whisk together olive oil, lemon juice, and black pepper.

3. Pour the dressing over the salad, tossing to coat.
4. Serve immediately or let it chill for 10 minutes.

TIPS & MODIFICATIONS: For a Greek-inspired flavor, add a dash of oregano. Store in an airtight container in the refrigerator for up to 2 days.

Nutritional Breakdown (per serving):
Protein: 5g, Potassium: 180 mg, Sodium: 10 mg, Fiber: 4g, Healthy Fats: 7g

Avocado & Cabbage Slaw with Fresh Herbs

Preparation Time: 10 minutes | **Serving Size:** 2

INGREDIENTS:
- 1 cup green cabbage, thinly sliced
- 1/2 ripe avocado, diced
- 1/4 cup fresh cilantro, chopped
- 1/4 cup fresh parsley, chopped
- 1 tablespoon olive oil
- 1 tablespoon lime juice
- Freshly ground black pepper, to taste

INSTRUCTIONS:
1. In a salad bowl, combine cabbage, avocado, cilantro, and parsley.
2. In a small bowl, whisk together olive oil, lime juice, and black pepper.
3. Drizzle the dressing over the slaw, tossing gently to coat.
4. Serve immediately to enjoy the fresh flavors.

TIPS & MODIFICATIONS: For extra texture, add sliced radishes or shredded carrots. Store without avocado for up to a day in the refrigerator to keep the slaw fresh.

Nutritional Breakdown (per serving):
Protein: 2g, Potassium: 120 mg, Sodium: 5 mg, Fiber: 5g, Healthy Fats: 10g

Comforting Carrot & Cauliflower Soup

Cooking Time: *30 minutes* | ***Preparation Time:*** *10 minutes* | ***Serving Size:*** *4*

INGREDIENTS:
- 1 tablespoon olive oil
- 1 small onion, chopped
- 2 cloves garlic, minced
- 4 medium carrots, chopped
- 1/2 head of cauliflower, chopped
- 4 cups low-sodium vegetable broth
- 1/2 teaspoon dried thyme
- Freshly ground black pepper, to taste
- Fresh parsley, chopped (for garnish)

INSTRUCTIONS:
1. Heat olive oil in a large pot over medium heat. Add the onion and garlic, cooking until softened, about 5 minutes.
2. Add carrots and cauliflower, stirring to coat with oil and cook for 3-5 minutes until slightly softened.
3. Add the vegetable broth, thyme, and black pepper. Bring the mixture to a boil, then reduce the heat and simmer for about 20 minutes, or until the vegetables are tender.
4. Using an immersion blender, puree the soup until smooth (or transfer to a blender in batches).
5. Garnish with fresh parsley before serving.

TIPS & MODIFICATIONS:
For a creamier texture, stir in 1/4 cup of unsweetened almond milk. Leftovers can be stored in an airtight container in the refrigerator for up to 3 days. Reheat gently over low heat on the stovetop.

Nutritional Breakdown (per serving):
Protein: 2g, Potassium: 170 mg, Sodium: 15 mg, Fiber: 3g, Healthy Fats: 3g

Herbed Vegetable & Barley Stew

Cooking Time: 45 minutes | **Preparation Time:** 10 minutes | **Serving Size:** 4

INGREDIENTS:
- 1 tablespoon olive oil
- 1 small onion, chopped
- 2 celery stalks, chopped
- 2 cloves garlic, minced
- 1/2 cup carrots, diced
- 1/2 cup zucchini, diced
- 1/4 cup pearled barley
- 4 cups low-sodium vegetable broth
- 1/2 teaspoon dried rosemary
- 1/2 teaspoon dried thyme
- Freshly ground black pepper, to taste

INSTRUCTIONS:
1. In a large pot, heat olive oil over medium heat. Add onion, celery, and garlic, cooking until softened, about 5 minutes.
2. Stir in carrots, zucchini, and barley, coating them with the oil.
3. Pour in the vegetable broth and add rosemary, thyme, and black pepper.
4. Bring the stew to a boil, then reduce the heat and let it simmer for 35 minutes or until the barley is tender.
5. Serve warm and enjoy the comforting flavors.

TIPS & MODIFICATIONS:
Add a handful of chopped fresh spinach at the end for extra nutrients. This stew can be stored in the refrigerator for up to 3 days or frozen for up to a month.

Nutritional Breakdown (per serving):
Protein: 3g, Potassium: 160 mg, Sodium: 20 mg, Fiber: 4g, Healthy Fats: 3g

Ginger-Infused Butternut Squash Soup

Cooking Time: 35 minutes | **Preparation Time:** 10 minutes | **Serving Size:** 4

INGREDIENTS:
- 1 tablespoon olive oil
- 1 small onion, chopped
- 1 tablespoon fresh ginger, grated
- 4 cups butternut squash, peeled and cubed
- 4 cups low-sodium vegetable broth
- Freshly ground black pepper, to taste
- 1/2 teaspoon ground cinnamon
- Fresh parsley, chopped (for garnish)

INSTRUCTIONS:
1. In a large pot, heat olive oil over medium heat. Add onion and ginger, cooking until fragrant, about 5 minutes.
2. Add butternut squash, stirring to coat with the ginger and onion. Cook for 3-4 minutes.
3. Pour in the vegetable broth and season with black pepper and cinnamon. Bring the mixture to a boil, then reduce the heat and simmer for 25 minutes, or until the squash is tender.
4. Use an immersion blender to puree the soup until smooth, or blend in batches.
5. Garnish with fresh parsley before serving.

TIPS & MODIFICATIONS:
For a creamy texture, stir in 1/4 cup of unsweetened almond milk. This soup can be stored in the refrigerator for up to 3 days or frozen for longer shelf life.

Nutritional Breakdown (per serving):
Protein: 2g, Potassium: 180 mg, Sodium: 15 mg, Fiber: 3g, Healthy Fats: 3g

No-Salt Minestrone Soup

Cooking Time: 40 minutes | **Preparation Time:** 10 minutes | **Serving Size:** 4

INGREDIENTS:
- 1 tablespoon olive oil
- 1 small onion, diced
- 2 cloves garlic, minced
- 1/2 cup celery, chopped
- 1/2 cup zucchini, diced
- 1/2 cup green beans, cut into 1-inch pieces
- 4 cups low-sodium vegetable broth
- 1/2 teaspoon dried basil
- 1/2 teaspoon dried oregano
- Freshly ground black pepper, to taste
- 1/2 cup cooked pasta shells (optional)

INSTRUCTIONS:
1. Heat olive oil in a large pot over medium heat. Add onion and garlic, cooking until softened and fragrant, about 5 minutes.
2. Stir in celery, zucchini, and green beans, cooking for another 3 minutes.
3. Pour in the vegetable broth, then add basil, oregano, and black pepper. Bring to a boil, then lower the heat and let it simmer for 30 minutes.
4. Stir in cooked pasta shells, if using, and cook for an additional 5 minutes.
5. Serve hot, garnished with fresh herbs if desired.

TIPS & MODIFICATIONS:
Add low-potassium vegetables like bell peppers or cabbage for added flavor. Store in the refrigerator for up to 3 days or freeze for a longer period.

Nutritional Breakdown (per serving):
Protein: 3g, Potassium: 150 mg, Sodium: 10 mg, Fiber: 4g, Healthy Fats: 3g

Simple Sweet Potato & Leek Soup

Cooking Time: 30 minutes | **Preparation Time:** 10 minutes | **Serving Size:** 4

INGREDIENTS:
- 1 tablespoon olive oil
- 1 small leek, cleaned and sliced
- 2 cups sweet potatoes, peeled and cubed
- 4 cups low-sodium vegetable broth
- 1/2 teaspoon ground cumin
- Freshly ground black pepper, to taste

INSTRUCTIONS:
1. In a large pot, heat olive oil over medium heat. Add sliced leeks and cook until soft, about 5 minutes.
2. Add sweet potatoes, stirring to coat them in the oil and leeks.
3. Pour in the vegetable broth, add cumin, and season with black pepper.
4. Bring to a boil, then reduce the heat and simmer for 25 minutes, until sweet potatoes are tender.
5. Use an immersion blender to puree the soup, or transfer in batches to a blender. Serve hot.

TIPS & MODIFICATIONS:
For a creamier consistency, blend in a handful of cooked white rice. Store leftovers in the refrigerator for up to 3 days or freeze for up to a month.

Nutritional Breakdown (per serving):
Protein: 2g, Potassium: 140 mg, Sodium: 10 mg, Fiber: 3g, Healthy Fats: 3g

Hummus & Veggie Wrap with Crunchy Cabbage

Preparation Time: 10 minutes | **Serving Size:** 1 wrap

INGREDIENTS:
- 1 large whole wheat tortilla
- 2 tablespoons kidney-friendly hummus (low-sodium)
- 1/4 cup shredded cabbage
- 1/4 cup cucumber, thinly sliced
- 1/4 cup grated carrots
- 1 tablespoon fresh parsley, chopped
- 1 tablespoon pumpkin seeds (optional)

INSTRUCTIONS:
1. Spread the hummus evenly over the tortilla.
2. Layer cabbage, cucumber, carrots, and parsley on top.
3. Sprinkle pumpkin seeds for added crunch, if desired.
4. Roll the tortilla tightly into a wrap, tucking in the sides as you go.
5. Slice in half and serve immediately.

TIPS & MODIFICATIONS:
Swap the tortilla for a low-sodium pita or lettuce wrap if preferred. For freshness, wrap tightly in parchment paper and refrigerate for up to 4 hours.

Nutritional Breakdown (per wrap):
Protein: 5g, Potassium: 160 mg, Sodium: 20 mg, Fiber: 4g, Healthy Fats: 6g

Herbed Chicken & Cucumber Sandwich

Cooking Time: 5 minutes (if using pre-cooked chicken) | ***Preparation Time:*** 10 minutes | ***Serving Size:*** 1 sandwich

INGREDIENTS:
- 2 slices kidney-friendly whole-grain bread
- 3 ounces cooked, shredded chicken breast
- 2 tablespoons Greek yogurt (unsweetened)
- 1/4 teaspoon dried dill
- 1/4 cup cucumber slices
- 1 tablespoon fresh parsley, chopped

INSTRUCTIONS:
1. In a small bowl, mix the chicken, Greek yogurt, and dill.
2. Layer the cucumber slices on one slice of bread, then spread the chicken mixture on top.
3. Sprinkle with parsley, then top with the second slice of bread.
4. Cut in half and enjoy.

TIPS & MODIFICATIONS: Replace the bread with a wrap or low-sodium bagel for variety. Store in an airtight container in the refrigerator for up to 6 hours.

Nutritional Breakdown (per sandwich):
Protein: 15g, Potassium: 200 mg, Sodium: 30 mg, Fiber: 5g, Healthy Fats: 3g

Egg White Salad Wrap with Fresh Dill

Cooking Time: 5 minutes | ***Preparation Time:*** 10 minutes | ***Serving Size:*** 1 wrap

INGREDIENTS:
- 1 large whole wheat tortilla
- 3 large egg whites, boiled and chopped
- 1 tablespoon Greek yogurt (unsweetened)
- 1/4 teaspoon fresh dill, chopped
- 1/4 cup shredded lettuce
- 1/4 cup grated carrots
- Freshly ground black pepper, to taste

INSTRUCTIONS:
1. In a bowl, mix the chopped egg whites, Greek yogurt, and dill.
2. Spread the egg mixture onto the tortilla.
3. Add lettuce and carrots on top.
4. Sprinkle with black pepper, then roll the tortilla tightly into a wrap.
5. Cut in half and serve.

TIPS & MODIFICATIONS:
For extra crunch, add a few slices of radish. Store wrapped in parchment paper in the refrigerator for up to 4 hours.

Nutritional Breakdown (per wrap):
Protein: 10g, Potassium: 180 mg, Sodium: 20 mg, Fiber: 3g, Healthy Fats: 2g

Roasted Red Pepper & Avocado Sandwich

Cooking Time: 5 minutes | ***Preparation Time:*** 10 minutes | ***Serving Size:*** 1 sandwich

INGREDIENTS:
- 2 slices kidney-friendly whole-grain bread
- 1/4 avocado, mashed
- 1/4 cup roasted red pepper slices (low-sodium, drained)
- 1 tablespoon fresh basil, chopped
- 1/4 cup spinach leaves

INSTRUCTIONS:
1. Spread the mashed avocado on one slice of bread.
2. Layer roasted red peppers and spinach leaves on top.
3. Sprinkle with fresh basil and cover with the second slice of bread.
4. Cut in half and enjoy.

TIPS & MODIFICATIONS:
For extra flavor, add a sprinkle of lemon juice. Store in an airtight container in the refrigerator for up to 4 hours.

Nutritional Breakdown (per sandwich):
Protein: 4g, Potassium: 180 mg, Sodium: 15 mg, Fiber: 5g, Healthy Fats: 8g

Turkey & Zucchini Wrap with Lemon Aioli

Cooking Time: 0 minutes (if using pre-cooked turkey) | **Preparation Time:** 10 minutes | **Serving Size:** 1 wrap

INGREDIENTS:
- 1 large whole wheat tortilla
- 2 ounces low-sodium turkey breast, thinly sliced
- 1/4 cup zucchini, thinly sliced
- 1 tablespoon Greek yogurt (unsweetened)
- 1/2 teaspoon lemon juice
- 1/4 teaspoon fresh thyme, chopped
- Freshly ground black pepper, to taste

INSTRUCTIONS:
1. In a small bowl, mix Greek yogurt, lemon juice, and thyme to make the aioli.
2. Spread the aioli over the tortilla.
3. Layer turkey slices and zucchini on top.
4. Sprinkle with black pepper, then roll the tortilla tightly into a wrap.
5. Slice in half and enjoy.

TIPS & MODIFICATIONS:
Use sliced bell peppers instead of zucchini for a variation. Wrap tightly in parchment paper for portability, and refrigerate for up to 4 hours.

Nutritional Breakdown (per wrap):
Protein: 12g, Potassium: 190 mg, Sodium: 25 mg, Fiber: 4g, Healthy Fats: 3g

Brown Rice & Broccoli Bowl with Miso Dressing

Cooking Time: 20 minutes | **Preparation Time:** 10 minutes | **Serving Size:** 1 bowl

INGREDIENTS:
- 1/2 cup cooked brown rice (low-sodium)
- 1/2 cup steamed broccoli florets

- 1 tablespoon miso paste (low-sodium)
- 1 tablespoon rice vinegar
- 1 teaspoon sesame oil
- 1/2 teaspoon honey
- 1 teaspoon sesame seeds
- Fresh parsley, chopped, for garnish

INSTRUCTIONS:
1. Cook the brown rice according to package instructions and steam the broccoli.
2. In a small bowl, whisk together miso paste, rice vinegar, sesame oil, and honey to create the dressing.
3. In a bowl, combine the cooked rice and steamed broccoli.
4. Drizzle the miso dressing over the rice and broccoli mixture.
5. Sprinkle sesame seeds and garnish with fresh parsley.
6. Serve warm or at room temperature.

TIPS & MODIFICATIONS:
For a different twist, try using quinoa or farro instead of brown rice. Keep leftovers in an airtight container in the refrigerator for up to 3 days.

Nutritional Breakdown (per bowl):
Protein: 6g, Potassium: 350 mg, Sodium: 200 mg, Fiber: 5g, Healthy Fats: 4g

Cilantro Lime Farro & Veggie Bowl

Cooking Time: 15 minutes | **Preparation Time:** 10 minutes | **Serving Size:** 1 bowl

INGREDIENTS:
- 1/2 cup cooked farro
- 1/4 cup cherry tomatoes, halved
- 1/4 cup cucumber, diced
- 1/4 cup red bell pepper, diced
- 1 tablespoon fresh cilantro, chopped
- 1 tablespoon lime juice
- 1 teaspoon olive oil
- Salt and pepper to taste

INSTRUCTIONS:
1. Cook the farro according to package instructions.
2. In a large bowl, combine the cooked farro, cherry tomatoes, cucumber, and bell pepper.

1. Drizzle with olive oil and lime juice, then toss in the chopped cilantro.
2. Season with salt and pepper to taste.
3. Serve immediately or chill for 30 minutes for a refreshing cold bowl.

TIPS & MODIFICATIONS: Feel free to swap farro with quinoa or brown rice, depending on your preference. Store leftovers in an airtight container in the refrigerator for up to 3 days.

Nutritional Breakdown (per bowl):
Protein: 8g, Potassium: 250 mg, Sodium: 10 mg, Fiber: 7g, Healthy Fats: 3g

Warm Quinoa Bowl with Spinach & Roasted Peppers

Cooking Time: 25 minutes | *Preparation Time:* 10 minutes | *Serving Size:* 1 bowl

INGREDIENTS:
- 1/2 cup cooked quinoa
- 1/2 cup fresh spinach leaves
- 1/4 cup roasted red bell peppers
- 1 tablespoon olive oil
- 1 tablespoon balsamic vinegar
- 1 teaspoon garlic powder
- Fresh basil, chopped, for garnish

INSTRUCTIONS:
1. Cook the quinoa according to package instructions and roast the bell peppers at 375°F for 20 minutes.
2. In a bowl, toss together the cooked quinoa, spinach, and roasted peppers.
3. Drizzle olive oil and balsamic vinegar over the mixture and sprinkle with garlic powder.
4. Toss to combine and garnish with fresh basil.
5. Serve warm.

TIPS & MODIFICATIONS: For added protein and crunch, sprinkle in some nuts or seeds. Store leftovers in an airtight container in the refrigerator for up to 3 days.

Nutritional Breakdown (per bowl):
Protein: 10g, Potassium: 330 mg, Sodium: 10 mg, Fiber: 6g, Healthy Fats: 6g

Wild Rice & Apple Salad with Maple Dressing

Cooking Time: 30 minutes | **Preparation Time:** 10 minutes | **Serving Size:** 1 bow

INGREDIENTS:
- 1/2 cup cooked wild rice
- 1/2 apple, thinly sliced
- 1/4 cup shredded carrots
- 1 tablespoon fresh walnuts, chopped
- 1 tablespoon maple syrup
- 1 tablespoon apple cider vinegar
- 1 teaspoon Dijon mustard

INSTRUCTIONS:
1. Cook the wild rice according to package instructions.
2. In a small bowl, whisk together maple syrup, apple cider vinegar, and Dijon mustard to make the dressing.
3. In a large bowl, combine the cooked wild rice, sliced apple, shredded carrots, and chopped walnuts.
4. Drizzle the maple dressing over the salad and toss to combine.
5. Serve immediately or refrigerate for 30 minutes for a chilled salad.

TIPS & MODIFICATIONS:
For an extra nutrient boost, add fresh spinach or kale. Store leftovers in an airtight container in the refrigerator for up to 2 days.

Nutritional Breakdown (per bowl):
Protein: 7g, Potassium: 300 mg, Sodium: 15 mg, Fiber: 6g, Healthy Fats: 5g

Barley & Cucumber Bowl with Lemon-Tahini Sauce

Cooking Time: 25 minutes | **Preparation Time:** 10 minutes | **Serving Size:** 1 bowl

INGREDIENTS:
- 1/2 cup cooked barley
- 1/4 cup cucumber, diced
- 1/4 cup cherry tomatoes, halved
- 1 tablespoon tahini
- 1 tablespoon lemon juice
- 1 teaspoon olive oil
- Fresh mint, chopped, for garnish

INSTRUCTIONS:
1. Cook the barley according to package instructions.
2. In a small bowl, whisk together tahini, lemon juice, and olive oil to create the dressing.
1. In a large bowl, combine the cooked barley, diced cucumber, and halved cherry tomatoes.
2. Drizzle the lemon-tahini sauce over the salad and toss to combine.
3. Garnish with fresh mint and serve.

TIPS & MODIFICATIONS:
For added protein, include grilled chicken or tofu. Store leftovers in an airtight container in the refrigerator for up to 3 days.

Nutritional Breakdown (per bowl):
Protein: 9g, Potassium: 260 mg, Sodium: 25 mg, Fiber: 7g, Healthy Fats: 6g

Grilled Chicken and Veggie Salad

Cooking Time: 15 minutes | **Preparation Time:** 10 minutes | **Serving Size:** 1 salad

INGREDIENT:
- 1 boneless, skinless chicken breast
- 2 cups fresh spinach
- 1/2 cucumber, sliced

- 1/2 cup cherry tomatoes, halved
- 1 tbsp olive oil
- 1 tsp lemon juice
- Salt and pepper (to taste)

INSTRUCTIONS:
1. Preheat the grill or a grill pan over medium-high heat.
2. Season the chicken breast with salt, pepper, and olive oil. Grill the chicken for 6-7 minutes on each side, or until fully cooked.
3. While the chicken is grilling, prepare the salad by placing spinach, cucumber, and cherry tomatoes in a large bowl.
4. Once the chicken is cooked, slice it into strips and add it to the salad.
5. Drizzle with lemon juice and a little more olive oil. Toss gently and serve immediately.

TIPS & MODIFICATIONS:
For extra flavor, try adding a few sprigs of fresh herbs like basil or parsley.
You can swap the chicken for grilled turkey breast for a leaner option.

NUTRITIONAL BREAKDOWN:
Protein: 30g, Fiber: 4g, Potassium: 350mg, Sodium: 120mg

Zucchini Noodles with Pesto

Cooking Time: 10 minutes | **Preparation Time**: 10 minutes | **Serving Size**: 1 serving

INGREDIENT:
- 2 medium zucchinis, spiralized into noodles
- 1/4 cup fresh basil leaves
- 1 garlic clove
- 1/4 cup olive oil
- 2 tbsp nutritional yeast
- Salt and pepper (to taste)

INSTRUCTIONS:
1. Use a spiralizer to turn zucchinis into noodles, or buy pre-spiralized zucchini noodles from the store.
2. In a food processor or blender, combine basil, garlic, olive oil, and

nutritional yeast. Blend until smooth.
3. Heat a non-stick skillet over medium heat. Add zucchini noodles and sauté for about 2-3 minutes, until slightly tender.
4. Toss the cooked zucchini noodles with the pesto sauce and season with salt and pepper.
5. Serve immediately as a light and flavorful lunch.

TIPS & MODIFICATIONS: Add a squeeze of lemon juice for extra freshness. You can add grilled chicken or shrimp to the dish for extra protein.

NUTRITIONAL BREAKDOWN:
Protein: 4g, Fiber: 3g, Potassium: 350mg, Sodium: 25mg

Lentil and Carrot Soup

Cooking Time: 30 minutes | **Preparation Time**: 10 minutes | **Serving Size**: 1 bowl

INGREDIENT:
- 1/2 cup dried lentils, rinsed
- 2 medium carrots, peeled and diced
- 1 small onion, chopped
- 2 garlic cloves, minced
- 4 cups low-sodium vegetable broth
- 1 tsp olive oil
- 1 tsp dried thyme
- Salt and pepper (to taste)

INSTRUCTIONS:
1. In a large pot, warm the olive oil over medium heat. Add the onion and garlic, and cook until they become soft, about 5 minutes.
2. Add carrots, lentils, vegetable broth, and dried thyme. Bring to a boil.
3. Reduce the heat and simmer for about 25-30 minutes, or until the lentils and carrots are tender.
4. Season with salt and pepper to taste.
5. Blend a portion of the soup with an immersion blender for a creamier texture, if desired.

6. Serve hot, garnished with a sprinkle of fresh herbs.

TIPS & MODIFICATIONS:
For extra flavor, try adding fresh parsley or dill as a garnish.
You can substitute lentils with other kidney-friendly beans like chickpeas.

NUTRITIONAL BREAKDOWN:
Protein: 15g, Fiber: 10g, Potassium: 600mg, Sodium: 150mg

Turkey Lettuce Wraps

Cooking Time: 15 minutes | **Preparation Time**: 5 minutes | **Serving Size**: 2 wraps

INGREDIENT:
- 1/2 lb lean ground turkey
- 2 garlic cloves, minced
- 1 tbsp fresh thyme or oregano
- 4 large lettuce leaves (romaine or butter lettuce)
- 1/2 avocado, sliced
- 1 tbsp olive oil
- Salt and pepper (to taste)

INSTRUCTIONS:
1. Warm olive oil in a skillet over medium heat. Add the ground turkey and cook until browned, about 5-7 minutes.
2. Stir in garlic, thyme, salt, and pepper. Cook for an additional 1-2 minutes until fragrant.
3. To serve, spoon the turkey mixture into the center of each lettuce leaf.
4. Top with slices of avocado and enjoy the wraps as a light, refreshing lunch.

TIPS & MODIFICATIONS:
Use other fresh herbs like cilantro or parsley for different flavors.
Add diced tomatoes or cucumber to the wraps for extra crunch.

NUTRITIONAL BREAKDOWN:
Protein: 25g, Fiber: 6g, Potassium: 450mg, Sodium: 200mg

Cucumber and Hummus Sandwiches

Cooking Time: 5 minutes | **Preparation Time**: 5 minutes | **Serving Size**: 1 sandwich

INGREDIENT LIST:
- 2 slices whole grain bread (low-sodium)
- 1/4 cup low-sodium hummus
- 1/2 cucumber, thinly sliced
- Fresh dill or parsley (optional)
- Salt and pepper (to taste)

INSTRUCTIONS:
1. Spread hummus evenly on both slices of whole grain bread.
2. Layer the cucumber slices on one slice of bread.
3. Sprinkle with salt, pepper, and fresh dill or parsley for added flavor.
4. Top with the other slice of bread, cut in half, and serve.

TIPS & MODIFICATIONS:
Add a few slices of tomato or avocado for extra creaminess.
Use gluten-free bread if needed for a gluten-free option.

NUTRITIONAL BREAKDOWN:
Protein: 8g | *Fiber*: 5g | *Potassium*: 250mg | *Sodium*: 130mg

Grilled Salmon with Asparagus

Cooking Time: 20 minutes | *Preparation Time*: 10 minutes | *Serving Size*: 1 plate

INGREDIENT LIST:
- 1 salmon fillet (about 6 oz)
- 1/2 bunch asparagus, trimmed
- 1 tbsp olive oil
- 1 tsp lemon juice
- Salt and pepper (to taste)

INSTRUCTIONS:
1. Preheat the grill to medium-high heat.
2. Drizzle the salmon fillet with olive oil, and season with salt and pepper.
3. Place the salmon on the grill and cook for about 4-6 minutes on each side, or until the fish flakes easily with a fork.
4. While the salmon is cooking, toss asparagus with olive oil, salt, and pepper, and grill for 4-5 minutes until tender.
5. Serve the salmon with grilled asparagus and drizzle with lemon juice.

TIPS & MODIFICATIONS:
For a variation, try serving with a side of quinoa or brown rice.
Add a pinch of garlic powder or fresh herbs like dill to the salmon for extra flavor.

NUTRITIONAL BREAKDOWN:
Protein: 30g | *Fiber*: 4g | *Potassium*: 600mg | *Sodium*: 180mg

Chapter 6: SATISFYING DINNERS

Zesty Lemon Herb Chicken with Roasted Veggies

Cooking Time: 40 minutes | **Preparation Time**: 15 minutes | **Serving Size**: 4 servings

INGREDIENTS:
- 4 boneless, skinless chicken breasts
- 1 large zucchini, sliced
- 1 medium red bell pepper, chopped
- 1 medium yellow bell pepper, chopped
- 1 cup sliced mushrooms
- 2 tablespoons olive oil
- Juice of 1 lemon
- 1 teaspoon dried oregano
- 1 teaspoon dried thyme
- Fresh parsley, chopped (for garnish)
- Black pepper to taste

INSTRUCTIONS:
1. Preheat the oven to 400°F (200°C).
2. Place the chicken breasts in a large bowl, add olive oil, lemon juice, oregano, thyme, and black pepper. Toss to coat.
3. Arrange the chicken breasts in the center of a sheet pan and surround with zucchini, bell peppers, and mushrooms.
4. Bake for 35-40 minutes or until chicken is cooked through and vegetables are tender.
5. Garnish with fresh parsley and serve warm.

TIPS & MODIFICATIONS:
Use fresh herbs like basil for added flavor without additional sodium.
Store leftovers in an airtight container for up to 3 days in the fridge.

Nutritional Breakdown (per serving):
Protein: 25g, Potassium: Low (specific levels vary by serving), Sodium: Low, Fiber: 3g, Healthy Fats: 8g

Garlic Butter Shrimp and Asparagus Sheet Pan

Cooking Time: 25 minutes, **Preparation Time**: 10 minutes, **Serving Size**: 4 servings

INGREDIENTS:
- 1 lb large shrimp, peeled and deveined
- 1 bunch asparagus, trimmed and cut into thirds
- 2 tablespoons unsalted butter, melted
- 3 cloves garlic, minced
- 1 tablespoon olive oil
- Fresh lemon wedges, for serving
- Black pepper to taste

INSTRUCTIONS:
1. Preheat the oven to 400°F (200°C).
2. In a large bowl, combine shrimp, melted butter, garlic, and black pepper.
3. Spread asparagus and shrimp evenly on a sheet pan and drizzle with olive oil.
4. Roast for 15-20 minutes or until shrimp are opaque and asparagus is tender.
5. Serve with a squeeze of lemon and enjoy.

TIPS & MODIFICATIONS: Substitute with green beans if asparagus is unavailable. Store any leftovers in the fridge for up to 2 days.

NUTRITIONAL BREAKDOWN (PER SERVING): Protein: 20g, Potassium: Low, Sodium: Low, Fiber: 2g, Healthy Fats: 6g

One-Pan Mediterranean Salmon with Olives & Veggies

Cooking Time: 30 minutes, **Preparation Time**: 10 minutes, **Serving Size**: 4 servings

INGREDIENTS:
- 4 salmon fillets
- 1 cup cherry tomatoes, halved

- 1/2 cup sliced black olives (low-sodium)
- 1 small zucchini, sliced
- 2 tablespoons olive oil
- 1 tablespoon fresh lemon juice
- 1 teaspoon dried basil
- Black pepper to taste

INSTRUCTIONS:
1. Preheat oven to 400°F (200°C).
2. Place salmon fillets on a large sheet pan, surround with cherry tomatoes, olives, and zucchini slices.
3. Drizzle with olive oil and lemon juice, sprinkle with dried basil and black pepper.
4. Bake for 25-30 minutes or until salmon flakes easily with a fork and vegetables are tender.

TIPS & MODIFICATIONS:
Swap salmon with tilapia or trout for variety.
Store leftovers in the fridge for up to 2 days.

Nutritional Breakdown (per serving):
Protein: 22g, **Potassium**: Low, **Sodium**: Low, **Fiber**: 3g, **Healthy Fats**: 10g

Baked Chicken Thighs with Sweet Potatoes & Green Beans

Cooking Time: 45 minutes, **Preparation Time**: 15 minutes, **Serving Size**: 4 servings

INGREDIENTS:
- 4 bone-in chicken thighs
- 1 large sweet potato, cubed
- 1 cup fresh green beans, trimmed
- 2 tablespoons olive oil
- 1 teaspoon dried rosemary
- Black pepper to taste

INSTRUCTIONS:
1. Preheat oven to 400°F (200°C).
2. In a large bowl, toss chicken thighs with olive oil, rosemary, and black pepper.
3. Place chicken on a sheet pan, surround with sweet

potato cubes and green beans.
4. Bake for 40-45 minutes or until chicken is golden brown and cooked through.

TIPS & MODIFICATIONS: Substitute with carrots if green beans aren't available. Leftovers can be stored in the fridge for up to 3 days.

Nutritional Breakdown (per serving):
Protein: 26g, Potassium: Low, Sodium: Low, Fiber: 4g, Healthy Fats: 8g

Easy Herb-Crusted Tilapia with Roasted Carrots & Peppers

Cooking Time: 25 minutes | *Preparation Time*: 10 minutes | *Serving Size*: 4 servings

INGREDIENTS:
- 4 tilapia fillets
- 1 large red bell pepper, sliced
- 1 cup baby carrots
- 2 tablespoons olive oil
- 1 teaspoon dried dill
- Black pepper to taste

INSTRUCTIONS:
1. Preheat oven to 400°F (200°C).
2. In a large bowl, coat tilapia with olive oil, dried dill, and black pepper.
3. Arrange tilapia on a sheet pan, surround with bell peppers and carrots.
4. Bake for 20-25 minutes or until tilapia flakes easily and veggies are tender.

TIPS & MODIFICATIONS:
- For variety, swap carrots with zucchini.
- Store leftovers in the fridge for up to 2 days.

Nutritional Breakdown (per serving):
Protein: 24g, Potassium: Low, Sodium: Low, Fiber: 3g, Healthy Fats: 7g

Whole Wheat Pasta Primavera with Garlic & Olive Oil

Cooking Time: 20 minutes | **Preparation Time**: 10 minutes | **Serving Size**: 4 servings

INGREDIENTS:

- 8 oz whole wheat pasta
- 1 medium zucchini, sliced
- 1 cup cherry tomatoes, halved
- 1/2 red bell pepper, sliced
- 1/4 cup olive oil
- 3 cloves garlic, minced
- Fresh basil leaves, chopped (for garnish)
- Black pepper to taste

INSTRUCTIONS:

1. Cook the pasta according to package directions, omitting any salt. Drain and set aside.
2. Heat olive oil in a large skillet over medium heat. Add garlic and sauté for 1-2 minutes until aromatic.
3. Add zucchini, cherry tomatoes, and red bell pepper to the skillet and cook until tender, about 5 minutes.
4. Combine the cooked pasta with the sautéed vegetables. Top with fresh basil and a sprinkle of black pepper.
5. Serve warm and enjoy.

TIPS & MODIFICATIONS:

- Substitute other kidney-friendly veggies like bell peppers or green beans if preferred.
- Leftovers can be stored in the fridge for up to 2 days.

Nutritional Breakdown (per serving):
Protein: 8g, Potassium: Low, Sodium: Low, Fiber: 6g, Healthy Fats: 10g

Quinoa-Stuffed Bell Peppers with Avocado Dressing

Cooking Time: 35 minutes | *Preparation Time*: 15 minutes | *Serving Size*: 4 servings

INGREDIENTS:
- 1 cup quinoa, rinsed
- 4 large bell peppers (any color), tops cut off and seeds removed
- 1 small zucchini, diced
- 1/2 cup diced carrots
- 1/2 teaspoon dried oregano
- Black pepper to taste
- 1/2 avocado
- 1 tablespoon olive oil
- Juice of 1 lime

INSTRUCTIONS:
1. Preheat oven to 375°F (190°C).
2. In a pot, cook quinoa according to package **INSTRUCTIONS**, then set aside.
3. In a large bowl, combine cooked quinoa, diced zucchini, carrots, oregano, and black pepper.
4. Stuff each bell pepper with the quinoa mixture, place on a baking sheet, and bake for 25-30 minutes.
5. Meanwhile, blend avocado, olive oil, and lime juice to create the dressing.
6. Drizzle the dressing over the stuffed peppers before serving.

TIPS & MODIFICATIONS:
- Use a red or yellow bell pepper to enhance the sweetness of the dish.
- Store leftovers in the fridge for up to 3 days.

Nutritional Breakdown (per serving):
Protein: 10g, Potassium: Low, Sodium: Low, Fiber: 7g, Healthy Fats: 6g

Lentil and Spinach Pasta in a Light Tomato Sauce

Cooking Time: 30 minutes, **Preparation Time**: 10 minutes, **Serving Size**: 4 servings

INGREDIENTS:
- 8 oz lentil pasta or whole wheat pasta
- 1/2 cup low-sodium tomato sauce
- 1 cup baby spinach leaves
- 1 tablespoon olive oil
- 1/2 teaspoon dried basil
- Black pepper to taste
- Fresh parsley, chopped (for garnish)

INSTRUCTIONS:
1. Cook pasta according to package directions, omitting any salt. Drain and set aside.
2. In a large skillet, heat olive oil over medium heat and add tomato sauce, basil, and black pepper. Simmer for 5-7 minutes.
3. Add baby spinach to the sauce and cook until wilted, about 2 minutes.
4. Toss pasta with the sauce, ensuring it's evenly coated. Garnish with parsley and serve warm.

TIPS & MODIFICATIONS:
Adjust the sauce thickness by adding a small amount of water if needed.
Store leftovers in an airtight container in the fridge for up to 2 days.

Nutritional Breakdown (per serving):
Protein: 12g, Potassium: Low, Sodium: Low, Fiber: 5g, Healthy Fats: 5g

Crispy Baked Rice with Veggies and a Lemon Vinaigrette

Cooking Time: 40 minutes | **Preparation Time**: 15 minutes | **Serving Size**: 4 servings

INGREDIENTS:
- 1 cup uncooked basmati rice
- 1 cup low-sodium vegetable broth
- 1/2 cup diced bell peppers
- 1/2 cup diced zucchini
- 1 tablespoon olive oil
- 1 teaspoon lemon zest
- 1 tablespoon lemon juice
- Black pepper to taste
- Fresh thyme (for garnish)

INSTRUCTIONS:
1. Preheat oven to 375°F (190°C).
2. In a baking dish, combine rice, vegetable broth, bell peppers, and zucchini. Cover with foil and bake for 30 minutes.
3. In a small bowl, whisk together olive oil, lemon zest, lemon juice, and black pepper to make a vinaigrette.
4. Once rice is cooked, drizzle the vinaigrette over it and garnish with fresh thyme.

TIPS & MODIFICATIONS:
- Use fresh parsley as an alternative garnish.
- Leftovers can be stored in the fridge for up to 3 days.

Nutritional Breakdown (per serving):
Protein: 6g, Potassium: Low, Sodium: Low, Fiber: 3g, Healthy Fats: 5g

Chickpea and Zucchini Pasta with Pesto Sauce

Cooking Time: 20 minutes | **Preparation Time**: 10 minutes | **Serving Size**: 4 servings

INGREDIENTS:
- 8 oz chickpea pasta
- 1 medium zucchini, spiralized or thinly sliced
- 2 tablespoons homemade low-sodium pesto (basil, olive oil, garlic, and black pepper)
- 1 tablespoon olive oil
- Black pepper to taste
- Fresh basil leaves (for garnish)

INSTRUCTIONS:
1. Cook chickpea pasta according to package directions, omitting salt. Drain and set aside.
2. In a large skillet, heat olive oil over medium heat and add zucchini. Sauté for 3-4 minutes until tender.
3. Toss pasta with zucchini and pesto until well coated. Season with black pepper.
4. Garnish with fresh basil leaves and serve.

TIPS & MODIFICATIONS:
Substitute zucchini with bell peppers or mushrooms if desired.
Store any leftovers in an airtight container in the fridge for up to 2 days.

Nutritional Breakdown (per serving):
Protein: 14g, Potassium: Low, Sodium: Low, Fiber: 7g, Healthy Fats: 8g

Grilled Salmon with Avocado Salsa

Cooking Time: 15 minutes | **Preparation Time**: 10 minutes | **Serving Size**: 4 servings

INGREDIENTS:
- 4 salmon fillets (4 oz each)
- 1 tablespoon olive oil
- Black pepper, to taste
- 1 avocado, diced

- 1/2 cup diced cucumber
- 1/2 cup diced tomatoes
- 1 tablespoon lime juice
- Fresh cilantro, chopped (for garnish)

INSTRUCTIONS:
1. Preheat grill to medium heat.
2. Brush each salmon fillet with olive oil and sprinkle with black pepper.
3. Grill salmon for 5-6 minutes per side, or until cooked through.
4. While salmon is grilling, mix avocado, cucumber, tomatoes, and lime juice in a bowl to create the salsa.
5. Serve the salmon with a spoonful of avocado salsa on top, garnished with fresh cilantro.

TIPS & MODIFICATIONS:
Substitute salmon with trout or another kidney-friendly fish if desired.
Store leftovers in the fridge for up to 2 days; salsa should be prepared fresh.

Nutritional Breakdown (per serving):
Protein: 22g, Potassium: Moderate, Sodium: Low, Fiber: 3g, Healthy Fats: 12g

Herb-Marinated Grilled Chicken with Spinach and Tomatoes

Cooking Time: 20 minutes | ***Preparation Time***: 15 minutes (plus 1 hour marination) | ***Serving Size***: 4 servings

INGREDIENTS:
- 4 boneless, skinless chicken breasts (4 oz each)
- 1/4 cup olive oil
- 1 tablespoon fresh thyme leaves, chopped
- 1 tablespoon fresh rosemary, chopped
- 1 clove garlic, minced
- Black pepper, to taste
- 2 cups fresh spinach
- 1 cup cherry tomatoes, halved

INSTRUCTIONS:
1. In a bowl, combine olive oil, thyme, rosemary,

garlic, and black pepper to make the marinade.
2. Add chicken to the marinade and let sit in the fridge for 1 hour.
3. Preheat grill to medium-high heat.
4. Grill chicken for 6-7 minutes on each side, or until fully cooked.
5. Sauté spinach and cherry tomatoes in a skillet until just wilted and serve alongside the grilled chicken.

TIPS & MODIFICATIONS:
Substitute fresh herbs with dried ones if needed.
Store any leftover chicken in the fridge for up to 3 days.

Nutritional Breakdown (per serving):
Protein: 24g, Potassium: Moderate, Sodium: Low, Fiber: 2g, Healthy Fats: 9g

Baked Cod with Garlic and Fresh Lemon

Cooking Time: 15 minutes | ***Preparation Time***: 10 minutes | ***Serving Size***: 4 servings

INGREDIENTS:
- 4 cod fillets (4 oz each)
- 1 tablespoon olive oil
- 2 cloves garlic, minced
- Zest of 1 lemon
- 1 tablespoon lemon juice
- Black pepper, to taste
- Fresh parsley, chopped (for garnish)

INSTRUCTIONS:
1. Preheat oven to 375°F (190°C).
2. Place cod fillets on a baking sheet lined with parchment paper.
3. In a small bowl, mix olive oil, garlic, lemon zest, lemon juice, and black pepper. Brush mixture over each fillet.
4. Bake cod for 12-15 minutes, or until it flakes easily with a fork.
5. Garnish with fresh parsley before serving.

TIPS & MODIFICATIONS:
Substitute cod with haddock or tilapia if desired.
Store any leftovers in an airtight container in the fridge for up to 2 days.

Nutritional Breakdown (per serving):
Protein: 20g, Potassium: Low, Sodium: Low, Fiber: 0g, Healthy Fats: 4g

Pan-Seared Chicken Breast with Roasted Brussels Sprouts

Cooking Time: 25 minutes | ***Preparation Time***: 10 minutes | ***Serving Size***: 4 servings

INGREDIENTS:
- 4 boneless, skinless chicken breasts (4 oz each)
- 1 tablespoon olive oil
- Black pepper, to taste
- 2 cups Brussels sprouts, halved
- 1 tablespoon balsamic vinegar
- Fresh thyme leaves (for garnish)

INSTRUCTIONS:
1. Preheat oven to 400°F (200°C).
2. Toss Brussels sprouts with half the olive oil and balsamic vinegar. Place on a baking sheet and roast for 20 minutes, until tender.
3. While Brussels sprouts are roasting, season chicken breasts with black pepper.
4. Heat remaining olive oil in a skillet over medium-high heat and sear chicken breasts for 6-7 minutes on each side, until cooked through.
5. Serve the chicken with roasted Brussels sprouts and garnish with fresh thyme.

TIPS & MODIFICATIONS:
Use cauliflower or broccoli instead of Brussels sprouts if preferred.
Leftovers can be stored in the fridge for up to 3 days.

Nutritional Breakdown (per serving):
Protein: 23g, Potassium: Moderate, Sodium: Low, Fiber: 3g, Healthy Fats: 6g

Citrus-Glazed Trout with Roasted Asparagus

Cooking Time: 20 minutes | **Preparation Time**: 10 minutes | **Serving Size**: 4 servings

INGREDIENTS:
- 4 trout fillets (4 oz each)
- 1/4 cup orange juice (freshly squeezed if possible)
- 1 tablespoon olive oil
- Black pepper, to taste
- 1 teaspoon orange zest
- 1 bunch asparagus, trimmed
- Fresh dill (for garnish)

INSTRUCTIONS:
1. Preheat oven to 400°F (200°C).
2. Place trout fillets on a baking sheet lined with parchment paper. Brush with olive oil and orange juice, and sprinkle with orange zest and black pepper.
3. Arrange asparagus on the same baking sheet, drizzling with a little extra olive oil if needed.
4. Roast for 15-20 minutes, until trout flakes easily with a fork and asparagus is tender.
5. Garnish with fresh dill and serve.

TIPS & MODIFICATIONS:
Substitute trout with tilapia or cod if preferred.
Store leftovers in an airtight container in the fridge for up to 2 days.

Nutritional Breakdown (per serving):
Protein: 21g, Potassium: Low, Sodium: Low, Fiber: 2g, Healthy Fats: 7g

Quinoa and Black Bean Veggie Burger Patties

Cooking Time: 25 minutes | **Preparation Time**: 15 minutes | **Serving Size**: 4 patties

INGREDIENTS:
- 1 cup cooked quinoa
- 1/2 cup canned low-sodium black beans, rinsed and mashed

- 1/4 cup grated carrots
- 1/4 cup finely diced bell pepper
- 1 tablespoon chopped fresh parsley
- 1/2 teaspoon cumin
- Black pepper, to taste
- 1/4 cup oat flour (or gluten-free flour of choice)
- 1 tablespoon olive oil (for cooking)

INSTRUCTIONS:
1. In a large bowl, combine the cooked quinoa, mashed black beans, carrots, bell pepper, parsley, cumin, black pepper, and oat flour. Mix until the ingredients come together.
2. Form the mixture into four patties.
3. Heat olive oil in a skillet over medium heat. Cook each patty for about 5 minutes on each side, until golden brown.
4. Serve with kidney-friendly toppings like lettuce, sliced cucumber, and a dollop of Greek yogurt if desired.

TIPS & MODIFICATIONS:
Store cooked patties in the fridge for up to 3 days or freeze for up to 1 month.
Substitute oat flour with chickpea flour for a higher protein option.

Nutritional Breakdown (per patty):
Protein: 7g, Potassium: Low, Sodium: Low, Fiber: 4g, Healthy Fats: 5g

Stuffed Acorn Squash with Brown Rice and Cranberries

Cooking Time: 45 minutes, **Preparation Time**: 10 minutes, **Serving Size**: 2 servings (1/2 squash per serving)

INGREDIENTS:
- 1 acorn squash, halved and seeds removed
- 1/2 cup cooked brown rice
- 1/4 cup dried cranberries
- 1/4 cup diced celery

- 1 tablespoon olive oil
- 1/2 teaspoon dried thyme
- Black pepper, to taste

INSTRUCTIONS:
1. Preheat oven to 400°F (200°C). Brush the cut sides of the acorn squash with olive oil and place cut-side down on a baking sheet.
2. Bake for 30 minutes, until tender.
3. In a bowl, mix the cooked brown rice, cranberries, celery, thyme, and black pepper.
4. Remove the squash from the oven and flip it over. Fill each half with the rice mixture.
5. Return to the oven for an additional 10 minutes.

TIPS & MODIFICATIONS:
- Substitute brown rice with quinoa or wild rice for variety.
- Refrigerate leftovers for up to 3 days.

Nutritional Breakdown (per serving):
Protein: 4g, Potassium: Low to moderate, Sodium: Low, Fiber: 6g, Healthy Fats: 7g

Sweet Potato and Lentil Shepherd's Pie

Cooking Time: 30 minutes | **Preparation Time**: 15 minutes | **Serving Size**: 4 servings

INGREDIENTS:
- 2 medium sweet potatoes, peeled and cubed
- 1 cup cooked lentils
- 1/2 cup diced carrots
- 1/2 cup diced celery
- 1/4 cup diced onion
- 1 tablespoon olive oil
- 1/2 teaspoon dried thyme
- Black pepper, to taste

INSTRUCTIONS:
1. Boil sweet potatoes in a pot of water until tender, about 10-12 minutes. Drain and mash until smooth.
2. Heat olive oil in a skillet over medium heat. Add carrots, celery, and onion, cooking until softened, about 5-7 minutes.

3. Add lentils, thyme, and black pepper to the skillet and stir.
4. Spread the lentil mixture evenly in a baking dish, then layer mashed sweet potatoes on top.
5. Bake at 375°F (190°C) for 15 minutes until golden on top.

TIPS & MODIFICATIONS:
- Substitute lentils with kidney-friendly mushrooms or chickpeas for a variation.
- Leftovers can be stored in the fridge for up to 3 days.

Nutritional Breakdown (per serving):
Protein: 8g, Potassium: Moderate, Sodium: Low, Fiber: 5g, Healthy Fats: 4g

Eggplant Parmesan with a Fresh Tomato Basil Sauce

Cooking Time: 35 minutes, **Preparation Time**: 15 minutes, **Serving Size**: 4 servings

INGREDIENTS:
- 1 large eggplant, sliced into rounds
- 1 cup low-sodium breadcrumbs
- 1/4 cup grated Parmesan (optional; kidney-friendly portions)
- 1 tablespoon olive oil
- 2 cups diced tomatoes
- 1/4 cup fresh basil, chopped
- Black pepper, to taste

INSTRUCTIONS:
1. Preheat oven to 400°F (200°C).
2. Coat each eggplant slice with breadcrumbs and arrange on a baking sheet. Drizzle with olive oil.
3. Bake for 20 minutes, flipping halfway.
4. Meanwhile, heat diced tomatoes in a skillet with black pepper until warmed through, about 5 minutes.

5. Remove eggplant from the oven and layer with tomato sauce and fresh basil. Sprinkle with Parmesan if desired and bake for an additional 10 minutes.

TIPS & MODIFICATIONS:
- For a vegan option, omit Parmesan or use a dairy-free alternative.
- Store leftovers in the fridge for up to 2 days.

Nutritional Breakdown (per serving):
Protein: 6g, Potassium: Low to moderate, Sodium: Low, Fiber: 4g, Healthy Fats: 6g

Chickpea & Spinach Stew with Turmeric and Cumin

Cooking Time: 20 minutes | *Preparation Time*: 10 minutes | *Serving Size*: 4 servings

INGREDIENTS:
- 1 cup canned low-sodium chickpeas, rinsed and drained
- 2 cups fresh spinach
- 1/2 cup diced carrots
- 1/2 cup diced bell pepper
- 1 tablespoon olive oil
- 1/2 teaspoon ground turmeric
- 1/2 teaspoon ground cumin
- Black pepper, to taste

INSTRUCTIONS:
1. Heat olive oil in a large pot over medium heat. Add carrots and bell pepper, cooking until softened, about 5 minutes.
2. Add chickpeas, turmeric, cumin, and black pepper, stirring to coat.
3. Add spinach and cook until just wilted, about 3 minutes.
4. Serve warm, garnished with additional black pepper if desired.

TIPS & MODIFICATIONS:
Substitute chickpeas with white beans for variety.
Store leftovers in the fridge for up to 3 days.

Nutritional Breakdown (per serving):
Protein: 7g, Potassium: Moderate, Sodium: Low, Fiber: 5g, Healthy Fats: 5g

Stuffed Bell Peppers with Quinoa and Turkey

Cooking Time: 30 minutes | ***Preparation Time***: 15 minutes | ***Serving Size***: 1 stuffed pepper

INGREDIENT LIST:
- 2 large bell peppers (any color)
- 1/2 cup quinoa, rinsed
- 1/2 lb lean ground turkey
- 1/2 cup diced tomatoes (no salt added)
- 1 tsp olive oil
- 1/2 tsp cumin
- 1/2 tsp paprika
- 1/4 tsp garlic powder
- Salt and pepper (to taste)

INSTRUCTIONS:
1. Preheat the oven to 375°F (190°C).
2. Cut the tops off the bell peppers and remove the seeds. Set aside.
3. In a medium pot, cook the quinoa according to package instructions.
4. While the quinoa is cooking, heat olive oil in a skillet over medium heat. Add ground turkey and cook, breaking it apart, until browned (about 5-7 minutes).
5. Stir in diced tomatoes, cumin, paprika, garlic powder, salt, and pepper, and cook for another 2-3 minutes.
6. Once the quinoa is cooked, mix it with the turkey mixture until well combined.
7. Stuff each bell pepper with the quinoa and turkey mixture. Place the stuffed peppers in a baking dish.
8. Cover with foil and bake for 20 minutes. Remove foil and bake for an additional 5-10 minutes, until peppers are tender.
9. Serve immediately.

TIPS & MODIFICATIONS:
You can add kidney-friendly vegetables like zucchini or mushrooms to the filling.
For a dairy-free version, omit any cheese or use a plant-based cheese substitute.

NUTRITIONAL BREAKDOWN:
Protein: 25g, Fiber: 6g, Potassium: 500mg, Sodium: 150mg

Baked Chicken with Rosemary and Lemon

Cooking Time: 35 minutes | *Preparation Time*: 10 minutes | *Serving Size*: 1 chicken breast with broccoli

INGREDIENT LIST:

- 1 boneless, skinless chicken breast
- 1 tsp fresh rosemary, chopped
- 1/2 lemon, sliced
- 1 tbsp olive oil
- 1 cup broccoli florets
- Salt and pepper (to taste)

INSTRUCTIONS:

1. Preheat the oven to 375°F (190°C).
2. Season the chicken breast with rosemary, lemon slices, olive oil, salt, and pepper.
3. Place the chicken on a baking sheet lined with parchment paper.
4. Arrange the broccoli florets around the chicken. Drizzle with a little olive oil and season with salt and pepper.
5. Bake for 25-30 minutes, or until the chicken reaches an internal temperature of 165°F (74°C) and the broccoli is tender.
6. Serve the chicken with the roasted broccoli on the side.

TIPS & MODIFICATIONS:
Add a sprinkle of grated Parmesan or nutritional yeast over the broccoli for extra flavor.
If you prefer, swap the broccoli for steamed green beans or asparagus..

NUTRITIONAL BREAKDOWN:

Protein: 30g, Fiber: 5g, Potassium: 400mg, Sodium: 150mg

Salmon and Veggie Foil Packets

Cooking Time: 25 minutes | *Preparation Time*: 10 minutes | *Serving Size*: 1 foil packet

INGREDIENT LIST:
- 1 salmon fillet (about 6 oz)
- 1 small zucchini, sliced
- 1/2 bell pepper, sliced
- 1/4 onion, thinly sliced
- 1 tbsp olive oil
- 1 tsp lemon juice
- Salt and pepper (to taste)

INSTRUCTIONS:
1. Preheat the oven to 400°F (200°C).
2. Place a large piece of aluminum foil on a baking sheet.
3. Lay the salmon fillet in the center of the foil.
4. Position the broccoli florets around the chicken, drizzle with olive oil, and season with salt and pepper.
5. Fold the sides of the foil up and over the fish and vegetables, sealing it into a packet.
6. Bake for 20-25 minutes, or until the salmon is cooked through and flakes easily with a fork.
7. Open the foil packet and serve immediately.

TIPS & MODIFICATIONS:
- Add fresh herbs like dill or parsley for a fresh flavor boost.
- Substitute salmon with a kidney-friendly fish like cod or tilapia.

NUTRITIONAL BREAKDOWN:
Protein: 30g, Fiber: 4g, Potassium: 550mg, Sodium: 180mg

Eggplant Parmesan (Low-Sodium)

Cooking Time: 45 minutes | **Preparation Time**: 20 minutes | **Serving Size**: 1 portion

INGREDIENT LIST:
- 2 medium eggplants, sliced into 1/4-inch rounds
- 1/2 cup whole wheat breadcrumbs (low-sodium)
- 1/2 cup part-skim mozzarella cheese, shredded
- 1 cup low-sodium marinara sauce
- 1 tsp olive oil
- 1/4 tsp garlic powder
- Fresh basil leaves for garnish
- Salt and pepper (to taste)

INSTRUCTIONS:
1. Preheat the oven to 375°F (190°C).
2. Place the eggplant slices in a single layer on a baking sheet. Lightly drizzle with olive oil and season with salt, pepper, and garlic powder.
3. Bake for 20 minutes, flipping halfway through, until the eggplant is tender.
4. In a baking dish, spread a small amount of marinara sauce on the bottom. Layer half of the baked eggplant slices, top with half of the marinara sauce, and sprinkle with mozzarella cheese.
5. Repeat the layers with the remaining eggplant, sauce, and cheese.
6. Bake for an additional 15-20 minutes, until the cheese is melted and bubbly.
7. Garnish with fresh basil and serve.

TIPS & MODIFICATIONS:
For added crunch, mix some crushed low-sodium crackers with the breadcrumbs.
Serve with a side of fresh greens or a simple salad.

NUTRITIONAL BREAKDOWN:
Protein: 12g, Fiber: 7g, Potassium: 600mg, Sodium: 250mg

Zucchini and Sweet Potato Fritters

Cooking Time: 15 minutes | **Preparation Time**: 10 minutes | **Serving Size**: 2 fritters

INGREDIENT LIST:
- 1 small zucchini, grated
- 1 small sweet potato, peeled and grated
- 1 egg, beaten
- 1/4 cup whole wheat breadcrumbs
- 1/4 tsp garlic powder
- 1/4 tsp paprika
- Salt and pepper (to taste)
- 1 tbsp olive oil

INSTRUCTIONS:
1. Grate the zucchini and sweet potato, then place them in a clean kitchen towel and squeeze out excess moisture.
2. In a bowl, combine the grated zucchini and sweet potato with the egg, breadcrumbs, garlic powder, paprika, salt, and pepper.
3. Heat olive oil in a non-stick skillet over medium heat.
4. Form the mixture into small patties and cook for 3-4 minutes on each side, until golden brown and crispy.
5. Serve immediately with a dollop of low-sodium yogurt or a fresh side salad.

TIPS & MODIFICATIONS: Add a pinch of dried herbs like thyme or oregano for added flavor.
You can substitute sweet potato with mashed pumpkin or carrot for a different flavor.

NUTRITIONAL BREAKDOWN:
Protein: 8g, Fiber: 6g, Potassium: 450mg, Sodium: 120mg

Cauliflower and Chickpea Stir-Fry

Cooking Time: 20 minutes | **Preparation Time**: 10 minutes | **Serving Size**: 1 serving

INGREDIENT LIST:
- 1 cup cauliflower florets
- 1/2 cup chickpeas (canned, drained, and rinsed)
- 1 tbsp olive oil
- 1 garlic clove, minced
- 1/2 tsp ground ginger
- 1/4 tsp turmeric
- 1/4 tsp cumin
- 1 tbsp low-sodium soy sauce
- 1/2 cup cooked quinoa

INSTRUCTIONS:
1. Warm olive oil in a large skillet over medium heat. Add garlic and sauté for 1 minute.
2. Add cauliflower florets and cook for about 5 minutes, stirring occasionally, until they start to soften.
3. Stir in the chickpeas, ginger, turmeric, cumin, and soy sauce, and cook for another 5-7 minutes, until the cauliflower is tender and the chickpeas are heated through.
4. Serve over a bed of cooked quinoa.

TIPS & MODIFICATIONS:
Add a squeeze of fresh lemon juice before serving for a tangy flavor.
Substitute chickpeas with kidney beans or lentils for a different texture.

NUTRITIONAL BREAKDOWN:
Protein: 12g, Fiber: 8g, Potassium: 600mg, Sodium: 220mg

Chapter 7: WHOLESOME SIDES AND SNACKS

Herbed Quinoa and Cucumber Salad

Cooking Time: 15 minutes
Preparation Time: 10 minutes
Serving Size: 4

INGREDIENTS:
- 1 cup quinoa, rinsed
- 1 ½ cups water
- ½ cucumber, diced
- ¼ cup fresh parsley, chopped
- ¼ cup fresh mint, chopped
- 1 tbsp olive oil
- Juice of 1 lemon
- Black pepper to taste

INSTRUCTIONS:
1. In a saucepan, combine quinoa and water. Bring to a boil, reduce heat, cover, and simmer for 15 minutes or until quinoa is cooked and fluffy.
2. In a mixing bowl, combine cooked quinoa with cucumber, parsley, mint, olive oil, lemon juice, and black pepper.
3. Toss well to blend flavors.

TIPS & MODIFICATIONS:
Enhance the flavor with a dash of lemon zest. Store leftovers in an airtight container in the fridge for up to 2 days.

Nutritional Breakdown (per serving):
Protein: 4g, Fiber: 5g, Sodium: 15mg, Potassium: 160mg, Healthy Fats: 5g

Garlic and Lemon Cauliflower Mash

Cooking Time: 20 minutes
Preparation Time: 5 minutes
Serving Size: 4

INGREDIENTS:
- 1 medium head of cauliflower, cut into florets
- 1 tbsp olive oil
- 1 clove garlic, minced
- Juice of ½ lemon
- Black pepper to taste

INSTRUCTIONS:
1. Steam cauliflower florets for about 15 minutes until tender.
2. Transfer to a food processor with olive oil, minced garlic, lemon juice, and black pepper. Blend until smooth and creamy.
3. Adjust seasoning to taste.

TIPS & MODIFICATIONS:
For a lighter texture, add a splash of unsweetened almond milk while blending. This mash can be stored for up to 3 days in the fridge.

Nutritional Breakdown (per serving):
Protein: 2g, Fiber: 4g, Sodium: 10mg, Potassium: 170mg, Healthy Fats: 4g

Fiber-Boosted Barley and Vegetable Pilaf

Cooking Time: 25 minutes
Preparation Time: 10 minutes
Serving Size: 4

INGREDIENTS:
- 1 cup pearled barley, rinsed
- 2 cups low-sodium vegetable broth
- 1 small zucchini, diced
- 1 small carrot, diced
- ¼ cup chopped parsley
- 1 tbsp olive oil

INSTRUCTIONS:
1. In a medium pot, combine barley and vegetable broth. Bring to

a boil, reduce heat, cover, and cook for 20 minutes.
2. In the last 5 minutes, stir in zucchini and carrots.
3. Remove from heat, drizzle with olive oil, and sprinkle with parsley.

TIPS & MODIFICATIONS: For extra color and flavor, add a pinch of turmeric. Store leftovers in the fridge for up to 3 days.

Nutritional Breakdown (per serving):
Protein: 6g, Fiber: 7g, Sodium: 20mg, Potassium: 150mg, Healthy Fats: 4g

Zesty Apple and Cabbage Slaw

Preparation Time: 10 minutes
Serving Size: 4

INGREDIENTS:
- 1 cup shredded green cabbage
- 1 small apple, julienned
- 2 tbsp apple cider vinegar
- 1 tbsp olive oil
- 1 tsp honey
- Black pepper to taste

INSTRUCTIONS:
1. In a large mixing bowl, combine cabbage and apple.
2. In a small bowl, whisk together apple cider vinegar, olive oil, honey, and black pepper.
3. Pour dressing over cabbage and apple, tossing to coat evenly.

TIPS & MODIFICATIONS: This slaw can be refrigerated for up to 2 days. Use pear or jicama in place of apple for variety.

Nutritional Breakdown (per serving):
Protein: 1g, Fiber: 3g, Sodium: 5mg, Potassium: 110mg, Healthy Fats: 4g

Savory Brown Rice with Fresh Herbs

Cooking Time: 25 minutes
Preparation Time: 5 minutes
Serving Size: 4

INGREDIENTS:
- 1 cup brown rice, rinsed
- 2 cups water
- ¼ cup chopped fresh parsley
- ¼ cup chopped fresh basil
- 1 tbsp olive oil

INSTRUCTIONS:
1. Combine brown rice and water in a medium pot. Bring to a boil, cover, and simmer for 25 minutes or until rice is tender.
2. Remove from heat and stir in parsley, basil, and olive oil.
3. Toss well to blend flavors.

TIPS & MODIFICATIONS:
For extra color and flavor, add a pinch of turmeric. Store leftovers in the fridge for up to 3 days.

Nutritional Breakdown (per serving):
Protein: 4g, Fiber: 3g, Sodium: 5mg, Potassium: 100mg, Healthy Fats: 4g

Crispy Zucchini Chips with Fresh Dill

Cooking Time: 25 minutes
Preparation Time: 10 minutes
Serving Size: 4

INGREDIENTS:
- 2 medium zucchinis, thinly sliced
- 1 tbsp olive oil
- 1 tsp dried dill
- ½ tsp garlic powder
- ¼ tsp black pepper

INSTRUCTIONS:
1. Preheat the oven to 375°F (190°C) and line a baking sheet with parchment paper.
2. Toss zucchini slices in olive oil, dill, garlic powder, and black pepper.

3. Arrange the zucchini slices in a single layer on the prepared baking sheet.
4. Bake for 20-25 minutes, flipping halfway through, until chips are golden and crispy.

TIPS & MODIFICATIONS:
For extra crunch, consider adding a sprinkle of Parmesan cheese before baking. These zucchini chips can be stored in an airtight container for up to 2 days.

Nutritional Breakdown (per serving):
Protein: 1g, Fiber: 2g, Sodium: 5mg, Potassium: 120mg, Healthy Fats: 5g

Cinnamon Spiced Apple Slices

Preparation Time: 5 minutes
Serving Size: 1

INGREDIENTS:
- 1 medium apple (such as Fuji or Gala), thinly sliced
- ½ tsp ground cinnamon
- 1 tsp honey (optional)

INSTRUCTIONS:
1. Core and slice the apple into thin wedges.
2. Sprinkle with cinnamon and drizzle with honey if desired.
3. Toss gently to coat, and enjoy immediately.

TIPS & MODIFICATIONS:
For added flavor, try sprinkling a bit of nutmeg or adding a few chopped nuts on top. These apple slices can be enjoyed fresh or stored for up to 1 day in the fridge.

Nutritional Breakdown (per serving):
Protein: 0g, Fiber: 4g, Sodium: 0mg, Potassium: 150mg, Healthy Fats: 0g

Blueberry Oat Energy Bites

Cooking Time: 10 minutes
Preparation Time: 10 minutes
Serving Size: 6 bites

INGREDIENTS:
- ½ cup rolled oats
- ¼ cup unsweetened dried blueberries
- 2 tbsp sunflower seeds
- 1 tbsp chia seeds
- 1 tbsp honey or maple syrup
- 1 tsp vanilla extract

INSTRUCTIONS:
1. In a mixing bowl, combine oats, dried blueberries, sunflower seeds, and chia seeds.
2. Add honey and vanilla extract and stir until fully combined.
3. Roll the mixture into 6 small balls (about 1 inch in diameter).
4. Chill in the refrigerator for at least 20 minutes before serving.

TIPS & MODIFICATIONS:
To make these energy bites more convenient, wrap each one individually in wax paper or plastic wrap. They can be stored in the fridge for up to one week.

Nutritional Breakdown (per serving):
Protein: 3g, Fiber: 4g, Sodium: 0mg, Potassium: 90mg, Healthy Fats: 3g

Cucumber Avocado Bites

Preparation Time: 5 minutes
Serving Size: 4

INGREDIENTS:
- 1 medium cucumber, sliced into rounds
- 1 ripe avocado
- ½ tsp lemon juice
- ¼ tsp black pepper

INSTRUCTIONS:
1. Slice the cucumber into rounds and set aside.
2. In a small bowl, mash the avocado and add lemon juice and black pepper.

3. Spoon the avocado mixture onto each cucumber round and serve.

TIPS & MODIFICATIONS:
For extra flavor, sprinkle with a pinch of paprika or chili powder. These bites are best enjoyed immediately but can be stored for a few hours in the fridge.

Nutritional Breakdown (per serving):
Protein: 1g, Fiber: 4g, Sodium: 5mg, Potassium: 200mg, Healthy Fats: 10g

Baked Cinnamon Squash Fries

Cooking Time: 30 minutes
Preparation Time: 10 minutes
Serving Size: 4

INGREDIENTS:
- 1 small butternut squash, peeled and cut into fries
- 1 tbsp olive oil
- 1 tsp ground cinnamon
- ½ tsp paprika
- ¼ tsp black pepper

INSTRUCTIONS:
1. Preheat the oven to 400°F (200°C) and line a baking sheet with parchment paper.
2. Toss squash fries in olive oil, cinnamon, paprika, and black pepper.
3. Arrange the fries in a single layer on the baking sheet.
4. Bake for 25-30 minutes, flipping halfway through, until fries are golden and tender.

TIPS & MODIFICATIONS:
For extra flavor, sprinkle with a pinch of paprika or chili powder. These bites are best enjoyed immediately but can be stored for a few hours in the fridge.

Nutritional Breakdown (per serving):
Protein: 1g, Fiber: 5g, Sodium: 5mg, Potassium: 150mg, Healthy Fats: 5g

Creamy White Bean and Basil Dip

Preparation Time: 10 minutes
Serving Size: 4

INGREDIENTS:
- 1 can (15 oz) white beans (like cannellini or navy beans), drained and rinsed
- 1 tbsp olive oil
- 2 tbsp fresh basil, chopped
- 1 tbsp lemon juice
- 1 clove garlic, minced
- ¼ tsp black pepper

INSTRUCTIONS:
1. In a food processor, combine the white beans, olive oil, basil, lemon juice, garlic, and black pepper.
2. Blend until smooth and creamy, scraping down the sides as needed.
3. Adjust seasoning to taste, adding more lemon juice or pepper if desired.
4. Serve with fresh vegetables or low-sodium crackers.

TIPS & MODIFICATIONS:
For an added kick, include a pinch of paprika or red pepper flakes. Store any leftovers in an airtight container in the refrigerator for up to 3 days.

Nutritional Breakdown (per serving):
Protein: 4g, Fiber: 4g, Sodium: 25mg, Potassium: 150mg, Healthy Fats: 5g

Zesty Herb Cottage Cheese Spread

Preparation Time: 5 minutes
Serving Size: 4

INGREDIENTS:
- 1 cup low-fat cottage cheese
- 1 tbsp fresh parsley, chopped
- 1 tbsp fresh chives, chopped
- ½ tsp lemon zest
- ½ tsp garlic powder
- ¼ tsp black pepper

INSTRUCTIONS:
1. In a bowl, combine cottage cheese, parsley, chives, lemon zest, garlic powder, and black pepper.
2. Stir until well mixed and creamy.
3. Serve with fresh cucumber slices, carrot sticks, or whole-grain crackers.

TIPS & MODIFICATIONS:
For extra creaminess, blend the cottage cheese in a food processor. This spread can be stored in the fridge for up to 2 days. Feel free to add other herbs like dill or thyme for variety.

Nutritional Breakdown (per serving):
Protein: 8g, Fiber: 1g, Sodium: 50mg, Potassium: 130mg, Healthy Fats: 2g

Classic Roasted Red Pepper Hummus

Cooking Time: 20 minutes
Preparation Time: 10 minutes
Serving Size: 4

INGREDIENTS:
- 1 jar (12 oz) roasted red peppers, drained
- 1 can (15 oz) chickpeas, drained and rinsed
- 1 tbsp tahini
- 1 tbsp olive oil
- 1 tbsp lemon juice
- 1 clove garlic, minced
- ¼ tsp cumin
- ¼ tsp paprika

INSTRUCTIONS:
1. Preheat the oven to 375°F (190°C). Place the red peppers on a baking sheet and roast for 10 minutes, or until they are slightly charred.
2. In a food processor, combine the roasted peppers, chickpeas, tahini, olive oil, lemon juice, garlic, cumin, and paprika.
3. Blend until smooth, adding a little water if needed for desired consistency.
4. Taste and adjust seasoning with more lemon juice or cumin if preferred.

5. Serve with sliced vegetables or low-sodium pita bread.

TIPS & MODIFICATIONS:
To make this dip spicier, add a pinch of cayenne pepper or chili flakes. This hummus can be stored in the fridge for up to 5 days.

Nutritional Breakdown (per serving):
Protein: 5g, Fiber: 4g, Sodium: 55mg, Potassium: 220mg, Healthy Fats: 7g

Lemon and Garlic Avocado Dip

Preparation Time: 5 minutes
Serving Size: 4

INGREDIENTS:
- 2 ripe avocados
- 1 tbsp lemon juice
- 1 clove garlic, minced
- ¼ tsp black pepper
- 2 tbsp fresh cilantro, chopped

INSTRUCTIONS:
1. In a bowl, mash the avocados until smooth.
2. Add lemon juice, garlic, black pepper, and cilantro, mixing well.
3. Taste and adjust seasoning with more lemon juice or pepper if desired.
4. Serve immediately with fresh vegetables, or refrigerate for up to 1 day.

TIPS & MODIFICATIONS:
To make the dip smoother, blend the ingredients in a food processor. You can also add a pinch of cumin or chili powder for extra flavor.

Nutritional Breakdown (per serving):
Protein: 2g, Fiber: 6g, Sodium: 5mg, Potassium: 350mg, Healthy Fats: 15g

Low-Sodium Greek Yogurt Herb Dip

Preparation Time: 5 minutes
Serving Size: 4

INGREDIENTS:
- 1 cup plain low-fat Greek yogurt
- 1 tbsp fresh dill, chopped
- 1 tbsp fresh parsley, chopped
- ½ tsp garlic powder
- ¼ tsp black pepper
- 1 tbsp lemon juice

INSTRUCTIONS:
1. In a bowl, combine Greek yogurt, dill, parsley, garlic powder, black pepper, and lemon juice.
2. Stir until well combined.
3. Adjust seasoning to taste.
4. Serve with fresh vegetables like carrots, celery, or bell peppers.

TIPS & MODIFICATIONS:
For a unique twist, add a pinch of dried oregano or some chopped chives. Store the dip in an airtight container in the fridge for up to 3 days.

Nutritional Breakdown (per serving):
Protein: 7g, Fiber: 1g, Sodium: 40mg, Potassium: 160mg, Healthy Fats: 2g

Roasted Carrot and Zucchini Medley

Cooking Time: 25 minutes
Preparation Time: 10 minutes
Serving Size: 4

INGREDIENTS:
- 3 large carrots, peeled and cut into 1-inch pieces
- 2 medium zucchinis, sliced into rounds
- 2 tbsp olive oil
- 1 tsp dried thyme
- ½ tsp black pepper
- 1 tbsp fresh parsley, chopped (optional)

INSTRUCTIONS:
1. Preheat the oven to 400°F (200°C).
2. In a bowl, toss the carrots and zucchinis with olive oil, thyme, and black

pepper until evenly coated.
3. Spread the vegetables in a single layer on a baking sheet.
4. Roast for 20-25 minutes, stirring halfway through, until the vegetables are tender and slightly caramelized.
5. Garnish with fresh parsley before serving.

TIPS & MODIFICATIONS: Try substituting zucchini with yellow squash for a different flavor. For extra seasoning, sprinkle garlic powder or paprika on the vegetables before roasting. Store any leftovers in the fridge for 2-3 days.

Nutritional Breakdown (per serving):
Protein: 2g, Fiber: 4g, Sodium: 50mg, Potassium: 400mg, Healthy Fats: 7g

Steamed Broccoli with Garlic and Lemon

Cooking Time: 10 minutes
Preparation Time: 5 minutes
Serving Size: 4

INGREDIENTS:
- 4 cups broccoli florets
- 1 tbsp olive oil
- 1 clove garlic, minced
- 1 tbsp lemon juice
- ¼ tsp black pepper

INSTRUCTIONS:
1. Steam the broccoli florets for 5-7 minutes until tender but still bright green.
2. While the broccoli is steaming, warm olive oil in a small pan over medium heat. Add the garlic and sauté for 1-2 minutes, or until aromatic.
3. Once the broccoli is done, toss it with the garlic oil, lemon juice, and black pepper.
4. Serve immediately as a side dish.

TIPS & MODIFICATIONS: For added flavor, sprinkle with grated parmesan or nutritional yeast. To make the meal more hearty, serve with whole grains like quinoa or brown rice. Leftovers can be stored in the refrigerator for up to 2 days.

Nutritional Breakdown (per serving):
Protein: 3g, Fiber: 4g, Sodium: 25mg, Potassium: 330mg, Healthy Fats: 4g

Spiced Roasted Sweet Potato Cubes

Cooking Time: 30 minutes
Preparation Time: 10 minutes
Serving Size: 4

INGREDIENTS:
- 3 medium sweet potatoes, peeled and cubed
- 2 tbsp olive oil
- 1 tsp ground cinnamon
- ½ tsp ground cumin
- ¼ tsp ground turmeric
- ¼ tsp black pepper

INSTRUCTIONS:
1. Preheat the oven to 400°F (200°C).
2. Toss the sweet potato cubes with olive oil, cinnamon, cumin, turmeric, and black pepper.
3. Spread the cubes on a baking sheet in a single layer.
4. Roast for 25-30 minutes, flipping halfway through, until tender and lightly browned.
5. Serve as a savory side dish.

TIPS & MODIFICATIONS:
You can add a pinch of chili powder or smoked paprika for a spicy kick. For an extra burst of flavor, squeeze fresh lime juice over the roasted sweet potatoes before serving. Leftovers can be stored in the fridge for 3 days.

Nutritional Breakdown (per serving):
Protein: 2g, Fiber: 5g, Sodium: 40mg, Potassium: 500mg, Healthy Fats: 7g

Sautéed Green Beans with Shallots

Cooking Time: 10 minutes
Preparation Time: 5 minutes
Serving Size: 4

INGREDIENTS:
- 4 cups fresh green beans, trimmed
- 1 tbsp olive oil
- 2 shallots, thinly sliced
- 1 tbsp lemon juice
- ¼ tsp black pepper

INSTRUCTIONS:
1. Heat olive oil in a large skillet over medium heat.
2. Add the sliced shallots and sauté for 2-3 minutes, until softened.
3. Add the green beans and cook for another 5-7 minutes, stirring occasionally, until the beans are tender.
4. Stir in lemon juice and black pepper, then remove from heat.
5. Serve warm as a flavorful side.

TIPS & MODIFICATIONS:
For extra flavor, add a handful of toasted almonds or sesame seeds. This dish pairs perfectly with lean proteins such as grilled chicken or fish. Leftovers can be stored in the refrigerator for up to 2 days.

Nutritional Breakdown (per serving):
Protein: 3g, Fiber: 4g, Sodium: 40mg, Potassium: 300mg, Healthy Fats: 5g

Lemon-Parsley Cauliflower Rice

Cooking Time: 10 minutes
Preparation Time: 5 minutes
Serving Size: 4

INGREDIENTS:
- 1 medium head of cauliflower, grated or processed into rice-like pieces
- 1 tbsp olive oil
- 1 clove garlic, minced
- 1 tbsp fresh parsley, chopped
- 1 tbsp lemon juice

- ¼ tsp black pepper

INSTRUCTIONS:
1. Grate or process the cauliflower florets into rice-like pieces.
2. Heat olive oil in a large skillet over medium heat. Add garlic and cook for 1 minute, until fragrant.
3. Add the cauliflower rice to the skillet and sauté for 5-7 minutes, until tender and slightly crispy.
4. Stir in lemon juice, fresh parsley, and black pepper.
5. Serve warm as a low-carb, flavorful side.

TIPS & MODIFICATIONS:
For added flavor, consider sprinkling in a pinch of ground turmeric or paprika. This dish pairs beautifully with grilled chicken or fish for a well-rounded meal. Leftovers can be stored in the fridge for up to 2 days.

Nutritional Breakdown (per serving):
Protein: 3g, Fiber: 4g, Sodium: 30mg, Potassium: 280mg, Healthy Fats: 5g

Crispy Baked Sweet Potato Fries

Cooking Time: 30 minutes
Preparation Time: 10 minutes
Serving Size: 1 cup of fries (about 10-12 fries)

INGREDIENT LIST:
- 2 medium sweet potatoes
- 1 tbsp olive oil
- 1/2 tsp cinnamon
- 1/2 tsp paprika
- Salt and pepper (to taste)

INSTRUCTIONS:
1. Preheat the oven to 425°F (220°C).
2. Peel and thinly slice the sweet potatoes into fries, ensuring uniform thickness for even baking.
3. In a bowl, toss the sweet potato fries with olive oil, cinnamon, paprika, salt, and pepper.
4. Spread the fries in a single layer on a baking sheet lined with parchment paper.

5. Bake for 25-30 minutes, flipping halfway through, until golden and crispy.
6. Serve immediately as a side dish or snack.

TIPS & MODIFICATIONS:
- For extra crispiness, use a wire rack on the baking sheet to allow air circulation around the fries.
- You can substitute sweet potatoes with carrots or zucchini for a different flavor profile.
- Store leftovers in an airtight container for up to 2 days, reheating in the oven for a crisp texture.

NUTRITIONAL BREAKDOWN:
Fiber: 4g, *Potassium*: 450mg, *Sodium*: 150mg, *Healthy Fats*: 5g (from olive oil)

Cucumber and Tomato Salad

Cooking Time: 10 minutes
Preparation Time: 10 minutes
Serving Size: 1 cup

INGREDIENT LIST:
- 1 large cucumber, sliced
- 2 medium tomatoes, diced
- 1/4 red onion, thinly sliced
- 1 tbsp fresh parsley, chopped
- 1 tbsp olive oil
- 1 tbsp lemon juice
- Salt and pepper (to taste)

INSTRUCTIONS:
1. In a large bowl, combine cucumber, tomatoes, red onion, and parsley.
2. In a small bowl, whisk together olive oil, lemon juice, salt, and pepper.
3. Pour the dressing over the vegetables and toss to combine.
4. Serve immediately or refrigerate for 30 minutes for flavors to meld.

TIPS & MODIFICATIONS:
Add fresh herbs like basil or mint for a refreshing twist. This salad pairs well with grilled chicken or fish.

Store leftovers in the fridge for up to 2 days in an airtight container.

NUTRITIONAL BREAKDOWN:
Fiber: 2g, Potassium: 300mg, Sodium: 120mg, Healthy Fats: 7g (from olive oil)

Roasted Garlic Cauliflower Bites

Cooking Time: 25 minutes
Preparation Time: 10 minutes
Serving Size: 1 cup of cauliflower bites

INGREDIENT LIST:
- 1 medium head of cauliflower, cut into florets
- 2 cloves garlic, minced
- 1 tbsp olive oil
- 1 tsp fresh rosemary, chopped
- Salt and pepper (to taste)

INSTRUCTIONS:
1. Preheat the oven to 400°F (200°C).
2. In a large bowl, toss the cauliflower florets with olive oil, minced garlic, rosemary, salt, and pepper.
3. Spread the cauliflower in a single layer on a baking sheet.
4. Roast for 20-25 minutes, flipping halfway through, until golden and crispy.
5. Serve as a savory snack or side dish.

TIPS & MODIFICATIONS:
- Add a sprinkle of Parmesan cheese or nutritional yeast for a cheesy flavor.
- Substitute rosemary with thyme or oregano for different herb flavors.
- Store leftovers in the fridge for up to 3 days and reheat in the oven.

NUTRITIONAL BREAKDOWN:
Fiber: 3g, *Potassium*: 400mg, *Sodium*: 150mg, *Healthy Fats*: 5g (from olive oil)

Kale Chips with Sea Salt

Cooking Time: 15 minutes
Preparation Time: 5 minutes
Serving Size: 1 serving (about 1 cup of chips)

INGREDIENT LIST:
- 1 bunch kale, washed and dried
- 1 tbsp olive oil
- 1/2 tsp sea salt

INSTRUCTIONS:
1. Preheat the oven to 350°F (175°C).
2. Tear the kale leaves into bite-sized pieces, removing the tough stems.
3. In a bowl, toss the kale with olive oil and sea salt.
4. Spread the kale in a single layer on a baking sheet.
5. Bake for 10-15 minutes, checking often, until the kale is crispy but not burnt.
6. Serve immediately as a crunchy snack.

TIPS & MODIFICATIONS:
Experiment with different seasonings such as garlic powder, smoked paprika, or lemon zest.
For a lower sodium option, skip the sea salt or use a salt substitute.
Store leftover kale chips in an airtight container for up to 2 days.

NUTRITIONAL BREAKDOWN:
Fiber: 2g, Potassium: 300mg, Sodium: 120mg, Healthy Fats: 4g (from olive oil)

Homemade Guacamole with Veggie Sticks

Cooking Time: 10 minutes
Preparation Time: 10 minutes
Serving Size: 1/4 cup guacamole with veggie sticks

INGREDIENT LIST:
- 2 ripe avocados, peeled and mashed
- 1 tbsp lime juice
- 1 tbsp fresh cilantro, chopped
- 1/4 tsp garlic powder
- Salt and pepper (to taste)

- Veggie sticks (carrots, celery, cucumber) for dipping

INSTRUCTIONS:
1. In a bowl, mash the avocados with a fork until smooth.
2. Add lime juice, cilantro, garlic powder, salt, and pepper, and mix until well combined.
3. Serve immediately with veggie sticks for dipping.

TIPS & MODIFICATIONS:
Add diced tomatoes or jalapeños for extra flavor.
Store guacamole in an airtight container with plastic wrap pressed directly onto the surface to prevent browning.
Veggie sticks can be prepped ahead of time and stored in the fridge for up to 3 days.

NUTRITIONAL BREAKDOWN:
Fiber: 5g, Potassium: 500mg, Sodium: 100mg, Healthy Fats: 20g (from avocados)

Apple and Almond Butter Slices

Preparation Time: 5 minutes
Serving Size: 1 apple, sliced (about 6-8 slices) with 1 tbsp almond butter

INGREDIENT LIST:
- 1 medium apple, sliced
- 1 tbsp almond butter
- A pinch of cinnamon (optional)

INSTRUCTIONS:
1. Slice the apple into thin wedges or rings.
2. Spread almond butter on each slice or serve on the side for dipping.
3. Optionally, sprinkle with a pinch of cinnamon for added flavor.
4. Serve immediately as a quick snack.

TIPS & MODIFICATIONS:
For a sweeter twist, drizzle with a little honey or maple syrup.
You can substitute almond butter with peanut butter or sunflower seed butter for variety.
Store leftover almond butter in a sealed container in the fridge for up to 1 week.

NUTRITIONAL BREAKDOWN:
Fiber: 4g, Potassium: 200mg, Sodium: 0mg, Healthy Fats: 8g (from almond butter)

Chapter 8: GUILT-FREE DESSERTS AND SWEET TREATS

Berry Coconut Parfait

Cooking Time: 0 minutes (No bake/cook)
Preparation Time: 10 minutes
Serving Size: 4

INGREDIENTS:

- 1 cup mixed berries (blueberries, strawberries, raspberries)
- 1 cup unsweetened coconut yogurt
- 2 tbsp shredded coconut (unsweetened)
- 1 tsp honey or maple syrup (optional)
- 1 tsp vanilla extract

INSTRUCTIONS:

1. Layer the coconut yogurt in the bottom of serving glasses.
2. Add a layer of mixed berries on top of the yogurt.
3. Repeat the layers, ending with a layer of berries on top.
4. Sprinkle with shredded coconut and drizzle with honey or maple syrup, if desired.
5. Chill in the refrigerator for 10-15 minutes before serving.

TIPS & MODIFICATIONS:
For extra sweetness, increase the amount of honey or use a sugar-free sweetener. Feel free to swap in any low-potassium berries you prefer. Leftovers can be stored in an airtight container in the fridge for up to 2 days.

Nutritional Breakdown (per serving):
Sugar: 9g, Fiber: 3g, Potassium: 150mg, Sodium: 20mg

Apple Cinnamon Delight Cups

Cooking Time: 15 minutes
Preparation Time: 10 minutes
Serving Size: 4

INGREDIENTS:
- 2 medium apples (peeled, cored, and chopped)
- 1 tsp ground cinnamon
- 1 tbsp honey or agave syrup
- ½ tsp vanilla extract
- ¼ cup unsweetened applesauce

INSTRUCTIONS:
1. In a small pot, combine the chopped apples, cinnamon, honey, and applesauce.
2. Cook over medium heat for 10-15 minutes, stirring occasionally, until the apples are tender.
3. Remove from heat and stir in vanilla extract.
4. Spoon the mixture into small cups or bowls and serve warm or chilled.

TIPS & MODIFICATIONS:
For a different twist, add a dash of nutmeg or ginger. For a creamier texture, top with a dollop of low-fat whipped cream or yogurt. You can store leftovers in the refrigerator for up to 2 days.

Nutritional Breakdown (per serving):
Sugar: 14g, Fiber: 4g, Potassium: 180mg, Sodium: 5mg

Chilled Pear Compote with Ginger

Cooking Time: 15 minutes
Preparation Time: 5 minutes
Serving Size: 4

INGREDIENTS:
- 3 pears, peeled, cored, and chopped
- 1 tsp fresh ginger, grated
- 2 tbsp honey or agave syrup
- 1 tsp lemon juice
- 1/4 tsp ground cinnamon

INSTRUCTIONS:

1. In a saucepan, combine the pears, ginger, honey, lemon juice, and cinnamon.
2. Cook over medium heat for 10-15 minutes, stirring occasionally, until the pears are soft and the mixture thickens.
3. Remove from heat and let cool to room temperature, then refrigerate for at least 30 minutes.
4. Serve chilled in small bowls or dessert cups.

TIPS & MODIFICATIONS: For a deeper flavor, add a splash of vanilla extract or use a mix of pears and apples. This dessert can be stored in the fridge for up to 3 days.

Nutritional Breakdown (per serving):
Sugar: 12g, Fiber: 4g, Potassium: 180mg, Sodium: 5mg

Blueberry Lemon Sorbet

Cooking Time: 0 minutes (No cook)
Preparation Time: 10 minutes
Serving Size: 4

INGREDIENTS:
- 2 cups fresh or frozen blueberries
- 2 tbsp lemon juice
- 2 tbsp honey or a sweetener of choice
- ½ cup water

INSTRUCTIONS:
1. In a blender, combine blueberries, lemon juice, honey, and water.
2. Blend until smooth.
3. Pour the mixture into a shallow dish and place it in the freezer.
4. Every 30 minutes, scrape the mixture with a fork to break up the ice crystals, repeating this process until the sorbet is fully frozen (about 3-4 hours).
5. Scoop into bowls and serve immediately.

TIPS & MODIFICATIONS: You can substitute other low-potassium berries like strawberries or raspberries. For a creamier version, blend in a little coconut milk before freezing. Store leftovers in an airtight container in the freezer for up to 1 week.

Nutritional Breakdown (per serving):
Sugar: 10g, Fiber: 2g, Potassium: 120mg, Sodium: 5mg

Grilled Pineapple Rings with Coconut Drizzle

Cooking Time: 10 minutes
Preparation Time: 5 minutes
Serving Size: 4

INGREDIENTS:
- 1 medium pineapple, peeled and sliced into rings
- 1 tbsp coconut oil
- 2 tbsp shredded coconut (unsweetened)
- 1 tsp honey or maple syrup (optional)

INSTRUCTIONS:
1. Preheat the grill or a grill pan to medium heat.
2. Brush the pineapple rings with melted coconut oil and place them on the grill.
3. Grill for 3-4 minutes per side, until grill marks appear and the pineapple softens slightly.
4. Drizzle with honey or maple syrup if desired and sprinkle with shredded coconut before serving.

TIPS & MODIFICATIONS:
For added flavor, sprinkle in some cinnamon or lime zest. For a creamier touch, serve with a dollop of coconut yogurt. Leftovers can be kept in the fridge for 1-2 days.

Nutritional Breakdown (per serving):
Sugar: 14g, Fiber: 2g, Potassium: 150mg, Sodium: 5mg

Cinnamon Apple Muffins with Oats

Cooking Time: 20-25 minutes
Preparation Time: 15 minutes
Serving Size: 12 muffins

INGREDIENTS:
- 1 ½ cups rolled oats
- 1 cup whole wheat flour
- 1 tsp baking powder
- 1 tsp ground cinnamon
- ½ tsp baking soda
- ¼ cup honey or maple syrup
- 1 egg (or egg substitute)
- 1 cup unsweetened applesauce
- ½ cup almond milk (or other non-dairy milk)
- 1 apple, peeled, cored, and chopped
- 1 tsp vanilla extract

INSTRUCTIONS:
1. Preheat the oven to 350°F (175°C). Line a muffin tin with paper liners or lightly grease it.
2. In a bowl, combine oats, whole wheat flour, baking powder, cinnamon, and baking soda.
3. In a separate bowl, whisk together honey, egg, applesauce, almond milk, and vanilla extract.
4. Add the wet ingredients to the dry ingredients and stir until just combined.
5. Gently fold in the chopped apple.
6. Divide the batter evenly into the muffin tin.
7. Bake for 20-25 minutes, or until a toothpick inserted into the center comes out clean.
8. Let the muffins cool before serving.

TIPS & MODIFICATIONS:
For added flavor, you can stir in chopped walnuts or raisins. Use gluten-free flour if needed. Store in an airtight container for up to 3 days or freeze for longer storage.

Nutritional Breakdown (per muffin):
Sugar: 8g, Fiber: 3g, Sodium: 30mg, Healthy Fats: 2g (from oats)

Honey-Sweetened Carrot Loaf

Cooking Time: 40-45 minutes
Preparation Time: 15 minutes
Serving Size: 10 slices

INGREDIENTS:
- 2 cups whole wheat flour
- 1 ½ tsp baking powder
- ½ tsp ground cinnamon
- ¼ tsp ground nutmeg
- 2 large eggs (or egg substitute)
- ¼ cup honey
- 1 tsp vanilla extract
- 1 ½ cups grated carrots
- ¼ cup unsweetened applesauce
- ¼ cup almond milk (or other non-dairy milk)

INSTRUCTIONS:
1. Preheat the oven to 350°F (175°C). Grease a loaf pan or line it with parchment paper.
2. In a bowl, whisk together whole wheat flour, baking powder, cinnamon, and nutmeg.
3. In another bowl, whisk together eggs, honey, vanilla extract, applesauce, and almond milk.
4. Add the wet ingredients to the dry ingredients and mix until just combined.
5. Fold in the grated carrots.
6. Pour the batter into the prepared loaf pan and smooth the top.
7. Bake for 40-45 minutes, or until a toothpick inserted into the center comes out clean.
8. Let the loaf cool in the pan for 10 minutes, then transfer to a wire rack to cool completely.

TIPS & MODIFICATIONS:
For added texture, stir in a handful of raisins or walnuts. To make it lower in carbs, substitute almond flour for whole wheat flour. Store in an airtight container for up to 3 days, or freeze for up to 1 month.

Nutritional Breakdown (per slice):
Sugar: 10g, Fiber: 4g, Sodium: 40mg, Healthy Fats: 4g (from almond milk)

Pumpkin Spice Cookies

Cooking Time: 10-12 minutes
Preparation Time: 10 minutes
Serving Size: 12 cookies

INGREDIENTS:
- 1 ½ cups almond flour
- ½ tsp baking soda
- 1 tsp ground cinnamon
- ½ tsp ground ginger
- ¼ tsp ground nutmeg
- ¼ cup honey or maple syrup
- ¼ cup pumpkin puree
- 1 egg (or egg substitute)
- 1 tsp vanilla extract
- ¼ cup coconut oil, melted

INSTRUCTIONS:
1. Preheat the oven to 350°F (175°C) and line a baking sheet with parchment paper.
2. In a bowl, combine almond flour, baking soda, cinnamon, ginger, and nutmeg.
3. In another bowl, whisk together honey, pumpkin puree, egg, vanilla extract, and melted coconut oil.
4. Add the wet ingredients to the dry ingredients and stir until just combined.
5. drop spoonfuls of dough onto the prepared baking sheet.
6. Bake for 10-12 minutes, or until the cookies are lightly golden and firm to the touch.
7. Let the cookies cool on the baking sheet for a few minutes before transferring to a wire rack.

TIPS & MODIFICATIONS:
For added crunch, try incorporating chopped walnuts or pumpkin seeds. If you prefer a sugar-free option, substitute with stevia. Store the cookies in an airtight container for up to 3 days, or freeze for up to 1 month.

Nutritional Breakdown (per cookie):
Sugar: 6g, Fiber: 2g, Sodium: 20mg, Healthy Fats: 7g (from coconut oil)

Banana-Blueberry Bites

Cooking Time: 10-12 minutes
Preparation Time: 5 minutes
Serving Size: 10 bites

INGREDIENTS:
- 1 ripe banana, mashed
- 1 cup rolled oats
- ½ cup blueberries (fresh or frozen)
- 1 tsp cinnamon
- ¼ cup unsweetened applesauce
- 1 tsp vanilla extract
- 2 tbsp chia seeds (optional)

INSTRUCTIONS:
1. Preheat the oven to 350°F (175°C) and line a baking sheet with parchment paper.
2. In a bowl, combine the mashed banana, oats, cinnamon, applesauce, and vanilla extract.
3. Gently fold in the blueberries and chia seeds (if using).
4. Scoop tablespoon-sized portions of the mixture and shape into small bites.
5. Place them on the prepared baking sheet and flatten them slightly.
6. Bake for 10-12 minutes, or until lightly golden on the edges.
7. Let the bites cool completely before serving.

TIPS & MODIFICATIONS:
Feel free to substitute other berries for blueberries, or add a spoonful of natural peanut butter for extra flavor. Store in an airtight container for up to 3 days or freeze for up to 1 month.

Nutritional Breakdown (per bite):
Sugar: 4g, Fiber: 3g, Sodium: 10mg, Healthy Fats: 2g (from chia seeds)

Almond Flour Shortbread Bars

Cooking Time: *18-20 minutes*
Preparation Time: *10 minutes*
Serving Size: *12 bars*

INGREDIENTS:
- 2 cups almond flour
- 1 tbsp honey or maple syrup
- 1 tsp vanilla extract
- ¼ tsp salt
- ¼ cup coconut oil, melted

INSTRUCTIONS:
1. Preheat the oven to 350°F (175°C). Line an 8x8-inch baking dish with parchment paper.
2. In a bowl, combine almond flour, honey, vanilla extract, and salt.
3. Add the melted coconut oil and stir until the mixture comes together into a dough.
4. Press the dough evenly into the prepared baking dish.
5. Bake for 18-20 minutes, or until the edges are golden brown.
6. Let the bars cool completely before cutting into squares.

TIPS & MODIFICATIONS:
For added flavor, sprinkle chopped nuts like almonds or walnuts on top before baking. Store in an airtight container for up to 5 days, or freeze for up to 1 month.

Nutritional Breakdown (per bar):
Sugar: 3g, Fiber: 2g, Sodium: 5mg, Healthy Fats: 9g (from coconut oil)

Tropical Mango Berry Bowl

Cooking Time: *5 minutes*
Preparation Time: *5 minutes*
Serving Size: *1 bowl*

INGREDIENTS:
- ½ cup frozen mango chunks
- ¼ cup frozen strawberries
- ¼ cup frozen blueberries

- ½ cup unsweetened coconut yogurt
- ¼ cup almond milk (or other kidney-safe non-dairy milk)
- 1 tbsp chia seeds
- 1 tbsp unsweetened shredded coconut (optional)
- Fresh mint for garnish (optional)

INSTRUCTIONS:
1. In a blender, combine frozen mango, strawberries, blueberries, coconut yogurt, and almond milk.
2. Blend until smooth and creamy. If needed, add more almond milk for desired consistency.
3. Pour the smoothie into a bowl.
4. Top with chia seeds, shredded coconut, and fresh mint.
5. Serve immediately.

TIPS & MODIFICATIONS:
For a sweeter bowl, drizzle with a bit of honey or maple syrup. Feel free to swap the fruit with other low-potassium options such as raspberries or blackberries. Store leftovers in an airtight container in the fridge for up to 24 hours.

Nutritional Breakdown (per serving):
Sugar: 15g, Fiber: 6g, Potassium: 200mg, Healthy Fats: 5g (from chia seeds and coconut)

Creamy Peach Smoothie Delight

Cooking Time: 5 minutes
Preparation Time: 5 minutes
Serving Size: 1 large glass

INGREDIENTS:
- 1 ripe peach, pitted and sliced
- ½ cup unsweetened coconut yogurt
- ½ cup almond milk
- 1 tbsp flaxseeds
- 1 tsp vanilla extract
- Ice cubes (optional)

INSTRUCTIONS:
1. Place the sliced peach, coconut yogurt, almond milk, flaxseeds, and vanilla extract into a blender.

2. Add ice cubes if desired for a thicker smoothie.
3. Blend until smooth and creamy.
4. Pour into a glass and serve immediately.

TIPS & MODIFICATIONS:
For extra sweetness, add a small drizzle of honey or agave. You can substitute the peach with nectarines or pears for variation. This smoothie is best consumed immediately, but leftovers can be stored for up to 24 hours in the fridge.

Nutritional Breakdown (per serving):
Sugar: 14g, Fiber: 5g, Potassium: 180mg, Healthy Fats: 3g (from flaxseeds)

Melon Mint Medley Bowl

Cooking Time: 5 minutes
Preparation Time: 10 minutes
Serving Size: 1 large bowl

INGREDIENTS:
- 1 cup cubed honeydew melon
- ½ cup cubed cantaloupe melon
- ¼ cup fresh mint leaves
- 1 tbsp unsweetened coconut flakes
- 1 tsp lime juice
- 1 tbsp pumpkin seeds

INSTRUCTIONS:
1. In a blender, combine honeydew melon, cantaloupe melon, and lime juice. Blend until smooth.
2. Pour the smoothie into a bowl.
3. Top with fresh mint leaves, coconut flakes, and pumpkin seeds.
4. Serve immediately, garnished with additional mint.

TIPS & MODIFICATIONS:
If the melon is too sweet, you can add a squeeze of lemon juice or a few extra mint leaves to balance the flavors. To add more texture, top with chopped almonds or sunflower seeds. Best when eaten fresh but can be stored

in the fridge for up to 24 hours.

Nutritional Breakdown (per serving):
Sugar: 20g, Fiber: 3g, Potassium: 300mg, Healthy Fats: 3g (from pumpkin seeds and coconut flakes)

Berry Almond Butter Smoothie

Cooking Time: 5 minutes
Preparation Time: 5 minutes
Serving Size: 1 large glass

INGREDIENTS:
- ½ cup frozen raspberries
- ½ cup frozen strawberries
- 1 tbsp almond butter (unsweetened)
- ½ cup almond milk (or other non-dairy milk)
- ½ tsp ground cinnamon
- 1 tsp honey (optional)

INSTRUCTIONS:
1. Add the frozen raspberries, strawberries, almond butter, almond milk, and ground cinnamon into a blender.
2. Blend until smooth and creamy, then add honey for extra sweetness, if desired.
3. Pour the smoothie into a glass and serve immediately.

TIPS & MODIFICATIONS:
For variety, try using sunflower seed butter or cashew butter in place of almond butter. To cut down on sugar, consider using a sugar substitute such as stevia. This smoothie is best enjoyed fresh, but can be stored in the fridge for up to 24 hours.

Nutritional Breakdown (per serving):
Sugar: 10g, Fiber: 7g, Potassium: 220mg, Healthy Fats: 9g (from almond butter)

Cucumber Kiwi Cool Smoothie

Cooking Time: 5 minutes
Preparation Time: 5 minutes
Serving Size: 1 large glass

INGREDIENTS:
- 1 small cucumber, peeled and chopped
- 2 ripe kiwis, peeled
- ¼ cup fresh mint leaves
- ½ cup coconut water
- 1 tsp lime juice
- 1 tsp honey or agave syrup (optional)

INSTRUCTIONS:
1. Combine the cucumber, kiwis, mint leaves, coconut water, lime juice, and honey/agave syrup in a blender.
2. Blend until smooth and creamy.
3. Pour the smoothie into a glass and garnish with additional mint leaves.
4. Serve immediately.

TIPS & MODIFICATIONS:
To reduce the natural sugar content, omit the honey or use a smaller portion of coconut water. For a thicker smoothie, add ice cubes or frozen cucumber slices. This smoothie is best when fresh but can be refrigerated for up to 24 hours.

Nutritional Breakdown (per serving):
Sugar: 12g, Fiber: 5g, Potassium: 250mg, Healthy Fats: 1g (from coconut water)

Coconut Cream Pudding with Maple

Cooking Time: 10 minutes
Preparation Time: 5 minutes
Serving Size: 1 bowl

INGREDIENTS:
- 1 cup full-fat coconut milk
- 2 tbsp maple syrup
- 2 tbsp cornstarch
- 1 tsp vanilla extract
- Pinch of salt

- Toasted coconut flakes for garnish (optional)

INSTRUCTIONS:
1. In a saucepan, combine the coconut milk, maple syrup, cornstarch, and a pinch of salt.
2. Stir the mixture over medium heat until it thickens, about 5-7 minutes.
3. Once thickened, remove from heat and stir in the vanilla extract.
4. Pour the pudding into individual serving bowls.
5. Refrigerate for 1-2 hours until set.
6. Garnish with toasted coconut flakes before serving.

TIPS & MODIFICATIONS:
For extra sweetness, add a little more maple syrup. You can also swap the coconut milk for almond or oat milk, but note that the flavor and texture may vary. Store in the fridge for up to 3 days.

Nutritional Breakdown (per serving):
Sugar: 9g (from maple syrup), Fiber: 2g, Potassium: 100mg, Sodium: 40mg

Vanilla Almond Chia Pudding

Cooking Time: 5 minutes
Preparation Time: 10 minutes (includes refrigeration)
Serving Size: 1 jar

INGREDIENTS:
- 1 cup unsweetened almond milk
- 3 tbsp chia seeds
- 1 tbsp honey or stevia (adjust to taste)
- ½ tsp vanilla extract
- 1 tbsp sliced almonds for garnish (optional)

INSTRUCTIONS:
1. In a bowl or jar, combine the almond milk, chia seeds, honey or stevia, and vanilla extract.
2. Stir well to ensure the chia seeds are evenly distributed.
3. Cover and refrigerate for at least 4 hours or overnight to allow the pudding to thicken.

4. Stir again before serving and top with sliced almonds.

TIPS & MODIFICATIONS:
For a different flavor, try adding a dash of cinnamon or a few mashed berries. You can substitute honey with agave or stevia to further reduce sugar. This pudding can be stored in the fridge for up to 3 days.

Nutritional Breakdown (per serving):
Sugar: 5g (from honey), Fiber: 6g, Potassium: 100mg, Sodium: 30mg

Honey Lemon Sorbet

Cooking Time: 10 minutes
Preparation Time: 15 minutes (plus freezing time)
Serving Size: 1 scoop

INGREDIENTS:
- 2 cups fresh lemon juice (about 6-8 lemons)
- ½ cup honey
- 1 cup water
- 1 tsp lemon zest
- Fresh mint leaves for garnish (optional)

INSTRUCTIONS:
1. In a small saucepan, combine water and honey. Heat over medium, stirring until the honey has fully dissolved. Remove from heat and allow to cool.
2. In a large bowl, mix the lemon juice and lemon zest with the cooled honey-water syrup.
3. Pour the mixture into a shallow baking dish or ice cream maker.
4. If using a baking dish, freeze for about 2-3 hours, stirring every 30 minutes to prevent ice crystals from forming.
5. Once frozen and fluffy, serve the sorbet in individual bowls or cones, garnished with fresh mint.

TIPS & MODIFICATIONS:
For added flavor, infuse the syrup with a sprig of rosemary or thyme before cooling. If you prefer a

sweeter sorbet, increase the honey. Store leftovers in an airtight container in the freezer for up to 1 week.

Nutritional Breakdown (per serving):
Sugar: 12g (from honey), Fiber: 1g, Potassium: 80mg, Sodium: 5mg

Cinnamon Pear Compote with Agave

Cooking Time: 15 minutes
Preparation Time: 5 minutes
Serving Size: 1 bowl

INGREDIENTS:
- 3 ripe pears, peeled and diced
- 1 tbsp agave syrup
- 1 tsp ground cinnamon
- ½ tsp vanilla extract
- ½ cup water
- Chopped walnuts for garnish (optional)

INSTRUCTIONS:
1. In a saucepan, combine the diced pears, water, agave syrup, and cinnamon.
2. Cook over medium heat, stirring occasionally, for about 10 minutes, until the pears are tender and the liquid has thickened.
3. Remove from heat and stir in the vanilla extract.
4. Serve warm or chilled, garnished with chopped walnuts.

TIPS & MODIFICATIONS:
For a richer flavor, add a pinch of nutmeg or cloves. You can substitute agave syrup with stevia or honey. This compote can be stored in the fridge for up to 3 days.

Nutritional Breakdown (per serving):
Sugar: 10g (from agave syrup), Fiber: 4g, Potassium: 160mg, Sodium: 5mg

Baked Apple Rings with Date Syrup

Cooking Time: 25 minutes
Preparation Time: 10 minutes
Serving Size: 2 apple rings

INGREDIENTS:
- 2 medium apples, cored and sliced into rings
- 2 tbsp date syrup
- 1 tsp ground cinnamon
- 1 tbsp crushed pecans (optional)

INSTRUCTIONS:
1. Preheat the oven to 350°F (175°C).
2. Place the apple rings on a baking sheet lined with parchment paper.
3. Drizzle the date syrup over the apple rings and sprinkle with cinnamon.
4. Bake for 20-25 minutes, until the apples are soft and slightly caramelized.
5. Serve warm, topped with crushed pecans if desired.

TIPS & MODIFICATIONS:
You can substitute date syrup with maple syrup or honey for a different flavor. For a crunchier texture, serve with a dollop of low-fat yogurt. These baked apple rings are best eaten fresh but can be stored in the fridge for up to 2 days.

Nutritional Breakdown (per serving):
Sugar: 12g (from date syrup), Fiber: 4g, Potassium: 180mg, Sodium: 5mg

Chilled Mango Coconut Sorbet

Cooking Time: 0 minutes (chilling time)
Preparation Time: 10 minutes
Serving Size: 1/2 cup

INGREDIENT LIST:
- 2 ripe mangoes, peeled and diced
- 1/2 cup coconut milk (full-fat or light)
- 1 tbsp honey or stevia (optional, depending on sweetness)
- 1/2 tsp lime juice (optional)

INSTRUCTIONS:
1. In a blender or food processor, combine the diced mango, coconut milk, honey or stevia, and lime juice (if using).
2. Blend until smooth and creamy.
3. Pour the mixture into a shallow dish or silicone mold, spreading evenly.
4. Freeze for at least 4 hours or until firm.
5. Scoop and serve chilled as a refreshing dessert.

TIPS & MODIFICATIONS:
You can use frozen mangoes for a quicker prep.
Adjust sweetness by adding more or less honey or stevia.
Store in the freezer for up to a week, but let it sit at room temperature for a few minutes before serving for easier scooping.

NUTRITIONAL BREAKDOWN:
Sugar: 15g (from mango and honey), **Fiber**: 2g, *Potassium*: 250mg, **Sodium**: 15mg, **Healthy Fats**: 6g (from coconut milk)

Baked Pears with Cinnamon and Walnuts

Cooking Time: 20 minutes
Preparation Time: 5 minutes
Serving Size: 1 pear

INGREDIENT LIST:
- 4 pears, halved and cored
- 2 tbsp honey
- 1/2 tsp cinnamon
- 1/4 cup walnuts, chopped
- 1 tsp olive oil (optional, for extra richness)

INSTRUCTIONS:
1. Preheat the oven to 375°F (190°C).
2. Place the pear halves in a baking dish, drizzling them with honey and sprinkling with cinnamon.
3. Top each pear with chopped walnuts and a small drizzle of olive oil (optional).
4. Bake for 18-20 minutes, until pears are tender and the walnuts are lightly toasted.
5. Serve warm as a cozy dessert.

TIPS & MODIFICATIONS: Substitute walnuts with pecans or almonds for a different texture.
You can add a scoop of vanilla yogurt or a dollop of whipped cream for extra indulgence.
Store leftovers in the fridge for up to 2 days and reheat before serving.

NUTRITIONAL BREAKDOWN:
Sugar: 12g (from pears and honey), **Fiber**: 5g, **Potassium**: 220mg, **Sodium**: 5mg, **Healthy Fats**: 7g (from walnuts and olive oil)

Chia and Almond Joy Pudding

Cooking Time: 0 minutes (overnight chilling time)
Preparation Time: 10 minutes
Serving Size: 1/2 cup

INGREDIENT LIST:
- 1/4 cup chia seeds
- 1 cup unsweetened almond milk
- 1 tbsp cocoa powder
- 1 tsp stevia or a low-potassium sweetener
- 2 tbsp unsweetened shredded coconut
- 1 tbsp almond butter

INSTRUCTIONS:
1. In a bowl, whisk together the chia seeds, almond milk, cocoa powder, and stevia until smooth.
2. Cover the bowl and refrigerate overnight (or for at least 4 hours) to let the pudding set.
3. Once ready to serve, stir the pudding and top with shredded coconut and almond butter.
4. Serve chilled as a creamy and indulgent dessert.

TIPS & MODIFICATIONS: Add a few drops of vanilla extract for extra flavor.
Use unsweetened coconut milk or another plant-based milk if preferred.
Store leftovers in the fridge for up to 3 days.

NUTRITIONAL BREAKDOWN:
Sugar: 2g (from almond milk and stevia), **Fiber**: 5g, **Potassium**: 150mg, **Sodium**: 50mg, **Healthy Fats**: 10g (from almond butter and coconut)

Banana Almond Ice Cream

Cooking Time: 5 minutes (blending)
Preparation Time: 5 minutes
Serving Size: 1/2 cup

INGREDIENT LIST:
- 2 ripe bananas, sliced and frozen
- 1 tbsp almond butter
- 1/2 tsp stevia or honey (optional)
- 1/4 tsp vanilla extract (optional)

INSTRUCTIONS:
1. Place the frozen banana slices into a blender or food processor.
2. Blend until smooth, scraping down the sides as needed.
3. Add almond butter, stevia (or honey), and vanilla extract, and blend until well combined.
4. Serve immediately as a soft-serve ice cream or freeze for 2-3 hours for a firmer texture.

TIPS & MODIFICATIONS:
- Add chocolate chips or a few berries for extra flavor and texture.
- For a dairy-free version, ensure the almond butter is free of added sugars.
- Store leftovers in an airtight container in the freezer for up to 1 week.

NUTRITIONAL BREAKDOWN:
Sugar: 14g (from bananas), **Fiber**: 3g, **Potassium**: 450mg, **Sodium**: 5mg, **Healthy Fats**: 8g (from almond butter)

Coconut-Lemon Energy Bites

Cooking Time: 0 minutes (no baking required)
Preparation Time: 10 minutes
Serving Size: 1 energy bite

INGREDIENT LIST:
- 1 cup shredded unsweetened coconut
- 1/4 cup almond flour
- 1 tbsp honey or stevia (optional)
- 1 tbsp lemon zest
- 1/4 tsp vanilla extract (optional)

INSTRUCTIONS:
1. In a bowl, combine shredded coconut, almond flour, honey (or stevia), lemon zest, and vanilla extract.
2. Mix until the **INGREDIENTS** are well incorporated.
3. Roll the mixture into small balls (about 1 inch in diameter).
4. Refrigerate for at least 30 minutes to firm up before serving.

TIPS & MODIFICATIONS:
- Add a pinch of sea salt for a sweet-salty combination.
- Store energy bites in the fridge for up to 1 week or freeze for longer storage.
- Substitute lemon zest with lime or orange zest for a different citrus flavor.

NUTRITIONAL BREAKDOWN:
Sugar: 4g (from honey), **Fiber**: 3g, **Potassium**: 150mg, **Sodium**: 5mg, **Healthy Fats**: 10g (from coconut and almond flour)

Strawberry Avocado Smoothie Bowl

Cooking Time: 0 minutes
Preparation Time: 5 minutes
Serving Size: 1 bowl (about 1 cup)

INGREDIENT LIST:
- 1 cup fresh strawberries, hulled
- 1/2 avocado, peeled and pitted
- 1/2 cup unsweetened almond milk
- 1 tbsp chia seeds
- 1 tbsp sliced almonds (for topping)
- 1 tsp honey or stevia (optional)

INSTRUCTIONS:
1. In a blender, combine strawberries, avocado, almond milk, chia seeds, and honey (if using).
2. Blend until smooth and creamy.
3. Pour into a bowl and top with sliced almonds.
4. Serve immediately as a refreshing smoothie bowl.

TIPS & MODIFICATIONS:
Top with fresh berries or coconut flakes for extra texture.
Adjust sweetness by adding more or less honey or stevia. Store leftovers in the fridge for up to 1 day, but it's best enjoyed fresh.

NUTRITIONAL BREAKDOWN:
Sugar: 7g (from strawberries and honey), **Fiber**: 6g, **Potassium**: 350mg, **Sodium**: 20mg, **Healthy Fats**: 15g (from avocado and almonds)

Chapter 9: HYDRATION AND BEVERAGES RECIPES

Cooling Cucumber Mint Water

Preparation Time: 5 minutes
Serving Size: 1 cup (about 8 oz)

INGREDIENTS
- 1/2 cucumber, sliced
- 5 fresh mint leaves
- 2 cups filtered water

INSTRUCTIONS
1. Add cucumber slices and mint leaves to a pitcher of filtered water.
2. Let it sit in the refrigerator for at least 2 hours to infuse the flavors.
3. Serve over ice if desired.

TIPS & MODIFICATIONS
- Add a splash of lemon juice for extra zest.
- For a stronger flavor, gently crush the mint leaves before adding.

Nutritional Breakdown (per cup)
Sugar: 0g, Fiber: 0g, Potassium: 10mg, Sodium: 0mg

Apple Cinnamon Infusion

Preparation Time: 5 minutes
Serving Size: 1 cup

INGREDIENTS
- 1/2 apple, thinly sliced
- 1 cinnamon stick
- 2 cups filtered water

INSTRUCTIONS
1. Add apple slices and cinnamon stick to a pitcher of water.
2. Refrigerate for 2-3 hours before serving.

TIPS & MODIFICATIONS
- Substitute a pinch of ground cinnamon if cinnamon sticks are unavailable.
- Use tart apples for a more tangy flavor.

Nutritional Breakdown (per cup)
Sugar: 1g, Fiber: 0g, Potassium: 15mg, Sodium: 0mg

Lemon and Basil Refreshment

Preparation Time: 5 minutes
Serving Size: 1 cup

INGREDIENTS
- 1/2 lemon, thinly sliced
- 4 fresh basil leaves
- 2 cups filtered water

INSTRUCTIONS
1. Add lemon slices and basil leaves to water.
2. Chill for 1-2 hours before drinking.

TIPS & MODIFICATIONS
- Adjust the lemon to taste; more slices add tartness.
- Try substituting mint for basil.

Nutritional Breakdown (per cup)
Sugar: 0g, Fiber: 0g, Potassium: 10mg, Sodium: 0mg

Strawberry Lime Splash

Cooking Time: 0 minutes
Preparation Time: 5 minutes
Serving Size: 1 cup

INGREDIENTS
- 3 strawberries, sliced
- 1/2 lime, thinly sliced
- 2 cups filtered water

INSTRUCTIONS
1. Combine strawberries and lime slices in water.
2. Let infuse in the refrigerator for at least 2 hours

TIPS & MODIFICATIONS
- For more flavor, muddle the strawberries slightly before adding them.
- Add ice for an extra refreshing touch.

Nutritional Breakdown (per cup)
Sugar: 1g, Fiber: 0g, Potassium: 15mg, Sodium: 0mg

Ginger and Pear Delight

Preparation Time: 5 minutes
Serving Size: 1 cup

INGREDIENTS
- 1/4 pear, thinly sliced
- 2 slices fresh ginger
- 2 cups filtered water

INSTRUCTIONS
1. Combine pear slices and ginger in water.
2. Chill for 3 hours to allow flavors to infuse.

TIPS & MODIFICATIONS
- Add more ginger for a spicier infusion.
- Pear adds a natural sweetness; no additional sweetener is needed.

Nutritional Breakdown (per cup)
Sugar: 0.5g, Fiber: 0g, Potassium: 10mg, Sodium: 0mg

Blueberry Orange Bliss

Preparation Time: 5 minutes
Serving Size: 1 cup

INGREDIENTS
- 1/4 cup blueberries
- 1/2 orange, thinly sliced
- 2 cups filtered water

INSTRUCTIONS
1. Add blueberries and orange slices to water.
2. Refrigerate for 2 hours before serving.

TIPS & MODIFICATIONS
- Squeeze some orange juice into the water for a stronger citrus flavor.
- For added sweetness, add a drop of stevia.

Nutritional Breakdown (per cup)
Sugar: 1.5g, Fiber: 0g, Potassium: 15mg, Sodium: 0mg

Pineapple Mint Cooler

Preparation Time: 5 minutes
Serving Size: 1 cup

INGREDIENTS
- 1/4 cup pineapple chunks
- 5 mint leaves
- 2 cups filtered water

INSTRUCTIONS
1. Add pineapple and mint to water.
2. Refrigerate for at least 2 hours.

TIPS & MODIFICATIONS
- For a stronger taste, muddle the pineapple pieces before adding.
- Substitute coconut water for added tropical flavor.

Nutritional Breakdown (per cup)
Sugar: 2g, Fiber: 0g, Potassium: 10mg, Sodium: 0mg

Watermelon Basil Tonic

Preparation Time: 5 minutes
Serving Size: 1 cup

INGREDIENTS
- 1/2 cup watermelon chunks
- 4 basil leaves
- 2 cups filtered water

INSTRUCTIONS
1. Place watermelon and basil in water.
2. Let infuse in the fridge for 2-3 hours before drinking.

TIPS & MODIFICATIONS
- Freeze watermelon cubes before adding for a chilled drink.
- Basil can be substituted with mint.

Nutritional Breakdown (per cup)
Sugar: 1g, Fiber: 0g, Potassium: 10mg, Sodium: 0mg

Cranberry Lime Infusion

Preparation Time*: 5 minutes*
Serving Size*: 1 cup*

INGREDIENTS
- 1/4 cup fresh or lightly crushed cranberries
- 1/2 lime, thinly sliced
- 2 cups filtered water

INSTRUCTIONS
1. Add cranberries and lime to water.
2. Refrigerate for at least 2 hours.

TIPS & MODIFICATIONS
- Crush cranberries for a stronger flavor.
- Lime can be swapped for lemon for a twist.

Nutritional Breakdown (per cup)
Sugar: 1g, Fiber: 0g, Potassium: 10mg, Sodium: 0mg

Apple Ginger Fizz

Preparation Time*: 5 minutes*
Serving Size*: 1 cup*

INGREDIENTS
- 1/2 apple, thinly sliced
- 2 slices fresh ginger
- 1 cup sparkling water
- 1 cup filtered water

INSTRUCTIONS
1. Add apple slices and ginger to a glass of water.
2. Let sit for 2 hours in the fridge, then top off with sparkling water before serving.

TIPS & MODIFICATIONS
Substitute sparkling water with coconut water for added flavor.
A pinch of cinnamon can enhance the apple flavor.

Nutritional Breakdown (per cup)
Sugar: 1g, Fiber: 0g, Potassium: 10mg, Sodium: 0mg

Peach and Lavender Refresher

Preparation Time: 5 minutes
Serving Size: 1 cup

INGREDIENTS
- 1/2 fresh peach, sliced
- 1/2 tsp dried lavender flowers
- 2 cups filtered water

INSTRUCTIONS
1. Add peach slices and lavender to a pitcher of water.
2. Allow it to chill for 1-2 hours in the refrigerator before serving.

TIPS & MODIFICATIONS
- For a stronger lavender flavor, add a few extra dried flowers.
- This drink pairs well with a squeeze of lemon if desired.

Nutritional Breakdown (per cup)
Sugar: 0.5g, Fiber: 0g, Potassium: 10mg, Sodium: 0mg

Melon Mint Sparkler

Preparation Time: 5 minutes
Serving Size: 1 cup

INGREDIENTS
- 1/4 cup honeydew melon, cubed
- 4 mint leaves
- 1 cup sparkling water
- 1 cup filtered water

INSTRUCTIONS
1. Add melon cubes and mint leaves to water.
2. Chill in the fridge for at least 2 hours, then top with sparkling water before serving.

TIPS & MODIFICATIONS
- Use frozen melon cubes for a colder drink.
- Substitute honeydew with cantaloupe if desired.

Nutritional Breakdown (per cup)
Sugar: 1g, Fiber: 0g, Potassium: 10mg, Sodium: 0mg

Pineapple Coconut Mocktail

Preparation Time: 5 minutes
Serving Size: 1 cup

INGREDIENTS
- 1/4 cup pineapple juice (unsweetened)
- 1/4 cup coconut water
- 1/2 cup filtered water
- Ice cubes (optional)

INSTRUCTIONS
1. Mix pineapple juice, coconut water, and filtered water in a glass.
2. Add ice cubes for a refreshing chill.

TIPS & MODIFICATIONS
- Add a sprig of mint for extra freshness.
- For more tropical flavor, add a slice of lime.

Nutritional Breakdown (per cup)
Sugar: 2g, Fiber: 0g, Potassium: 25mg, Sodium: 10mg

Raspberry Basil Twist

Preparation Time: 5 minutes
Serving Size: 1 cup

INGREDIENTS
- 1/4 cup raspberries
- 3-4 fresh basil leaves
- 2 cups filtered water

INSTRUCTIONS
1. Place raspberries and basil leaves in a pitcher of water.
2. Allow the flavors to infuse for at least 2 hours in the fridge.

TIPS & MODIFICATIONS
- Lightly crush the raspberries for a bolder flavor.
- Substitute basil with mint for a different taste.

Nutritional Breakdown (per cup)
Sugar: 0.5g, Fiber: 0g, Potassium: 10mg, Sodium: 0mg

Cucumber Lemon Spritzer

Preparation Time: 5 minutes
Serving Size: 1 cup

INGREDIENTS
- 1/4 cucumber, thinly sliced
- 1/2 lemon, thinly sliced
- 1 cup sparkling water
- 1 cup filtered water

INSTRUCTIONS
1. Combine cucumber and lemon slices in filtered water.
2. Allow to chill in the fridge for at least 2 hours.
3. Top with sparkling water before serving.

TIPS & MODIFICATIONS
- Add a sprig of mint for extra freshness.
- For more tropical flavor, add a slice of lime.

Nutritional Breakdown (per cup)
Sugar: 0g, Fiber: 0g, Potassium: 10mg, Sodium: 0mg

Berry-Ginger Smoothie

Preparation Time: 5 minutes
Serving Size: 1 cup

INGREDIENTS
- 1/4 cup blueberries
- 1/4 cup strawberries, hulled
- 1/2 cup unsweetened almond milk
- 1 slice fresh ginger

INSTRUCTIONS
1. Blend all ingredients until smooth.
2. Pour into a glass and serve immediately.

TIPS & MODIFICATIONS
- Substitute almond milk with oat milk for a creamier texture.
- Adjust sweetness by adding stevia if desired.

Nutritional Breakdown (per cup)
Sugar: 4g, Fiber: 2g, Potassium: 50mg, Sodium: 5mg

Mango Avocado Smoothie

Preparation Time: 5 minutes
Serving Size: 1 cup

INGREDIENTS
- 1/4 cup mango, cubed
- 1/4 avocado
- 1/2 cup unsweetened almond milk

INSTRUCTIONS
1. Blend mango, avocado, and almond milk until smooth.
2. Pour into a glass and serve immediately.

Nutritional Breakdown (per cup)
Sugar: 3g, Fiber: 3g, Potassium: 70mg, Sodium: 5mg

Apple Cinnamon Warm Drink

Cooking Time: 5 minutes
Preparation Time: 5 minutes
Serving Size: 1 cup

INGREDIENTS
- 1 cup water
- 1/4 apple, thinly sliced
- 1 cinnamon stick

INSTRUCTIONS
1. Add apple slices and cinnamon stick to a pot of water.
2. Bring to a simmer and let steep for 5 minutes.
3. Strain and serve warm.

TIPS & MODIFICATIONS
- Add a pinch of nutmeg for added warmth.
- Sweeten with a touch of honey if desired.

Nutritional Breakdown (per cup)
Sugar: 0.5g, Fiber: 0g, Potassium: 5mg, Sodium: 0mg

Ginger Lemon Herbal Tea

Cooking Time: 5 minutes
Preparation Time: 5 minutes
Serving Size: 1 cup

INGREDIENTS
- 1 cup water
- 2 slices fresh ginger
- 1/2 lemon, juiced

INSTRUCTIONS
1. Bring water to a boil and add ginger slices.
2. Let steep for 5 minutes, then add lemon juice.
3. Strain and enjoy warm.

TIPS & MODIFICATIONS
- Substitute lemon with lime for a different citrus taste.
- Add a few mint leaves for an extra refreshing flavor.

Nutritional Breakdown (per cup)
Sugar: 0g, Fiber: 0g, Potassium: 5mg, Sodium: 0mg

Chamomile Honey Tea

Cooking Time: 5 minutes
Preparation Time: 5 minutes
Serving Size: 1 cup

INGREDIENTS
- 1 cup water
- 1 chamomile tea bag
- 1 tsp honey (optional)

INSTRUCTIONS
1. Boil water and pour over the chamomile tea bag.
2. Steep for 3-5 minutes, then remove the tea bag.
3. Stir in honey if desired and serve warm.

TIPS & MODIFICATIONS
- Enjoy before bed for a calming effect.
- Add a dash of cinnamon for a warming flavor.

Nutritional Breakdown (per cup)
Sugar: 1g, Fiber: 0g, Potassium: 0mg, Sodium: 0mg

Chapter 11: KIDNEY-FRIENDLY AIR FRYER RECIPES

Air Fryer Cinnamon Apple Chips

Cooking Time: 15 minutes
Preparation Time: 5 minutes
Serving Size: 1/2 cup

INGREDIENT LIST:

- 2 medium apples (like Gala or Fuji)
- 1/2 tsp cinnamon
- 1/2 tsp stevia or honey (optional)

INSTRUCTIONS:

1. Preheat the air fryer to 300°F (150°C).
2. Core the apples, then slice them thinly with a mandoline or knife.
3. Place the apple slices in a bowl and sprinkle with cinnamon and stevia (if using), tossing to coat.
4. Arrange the apple slices in a single layer in the air fryer basket.
5. Air fry for 12-15 minutes, flipping halfway through, until the apple slices are crisp.
6. Let cool for a few minutes to allow them to crisp further, then serve.

TIPS & MODIFICATIONS:

- Substitute apples with pears for a different flavor.
- Adjust the sweetness by using more or less stevia or honey.
- Store in an airtight container at room temperature for up to 2 days.

NUTRITIONAL BREAKDOWN:
Sugar: 10g (from apples), **Fiber**: 3g, **Potassium**: 150mg, **Sodium**: 0mg

Air Fryer Coconut Macaroons

Cooking Time: 8 minutes
Preparation Time: 10 minutes
Serving Size: 1 macaroon

INGREDIENT LIST:

- 1 cup shredded unsweetened coconut
- 2 tbsp almond flour
- 2 tbsp honey or stevia
- 1 large egg white
- 1/2 tsp vanilla extract

INSTRUCTIONS:

1. In a bowl, mix together the shredded coconut, almond flour, honey or stevia, egg white, and vanilla extract until well combined.
2. Shape the mixture into small balls or mounds and place them on parchment paper.
3. Preheat the air fryer to 350°F (175°C).
4. Place the macaroons in the air fryer basket on parchment paper, making sure they're not touching.
5. Air fry for 6-8 minutes until golden brown. Allow to cool before serving.

TIPS & MODIFICATIONS:

- Substitute vanilla extract with almond or lemon extract for a flavor twist.
- For a chocolate version, dip the macaroons in melted dark chocolate.
- Store in an airtight container at room temperature for up to 3 days.

NUTRITIONAL BREAKDOWN:
Sugar: 3g (from honey), **Fiber**: 2g, **Potassium**: 80mg, **Sodium**: 10mg, **Healthy Fats**: 5g (from coconut and almond flour)

Air Fryer Baked Bananas with Cinnamon

Cooking Time: 6 minutes
Preparation Time: 2 minutes
Serving Size: 1/2 banana

INGREDIENT LIST:
- 2 bananas, peeled and halved lengthwise
- 1/2 tsp cinnamon
- 1 tsp honey or stevia (optional)

INSTRUCTIONS:
1. Preheat the air fryer to 375°F (190°C).
2. Sprinkle cinnamon over the banana halves and drizzle with honey or stevia if desired.
3. Place bananas in the air fryer basket with the cut side facing up.
4. Air fry for 5-6 minutes until golden and slightly caramelized.
5. Serve warm, optionally with a dollop of yogurt or a sprinkle of chopped nuts.

TIPS & MODIFICATIONS:
Add a sprinkle of chopped walnuts or almonds for a crunch.
For a tropical twist, drizzle with a small amount of coconut milk.
Enjoy immediately, as bananas may soften over time.

NUTRITIONAL BREAKDOWN:
Sugar: 9g (from banana), *Fiber*: 2g, *Potassium*: 200mg, *Sodium*: 0mg

Air Fryer Pineapple Rings with Honey

Cooking Time: 5 minutes
Preparation Time: 3 minutes
Serving Size: 2 pineapple rings

INGREDIENT LIST:
- 4 fresh pineapple rings (about 1/2 inch thick)
- 1 tbsp honey or stevia (optional)

- 1/4 tsp ground ginger (optional for a hint of spice)

INSTRUCTIONS:
1. Preheat the air fryer to 375°F (190°C).
2. Brush each pineapple ring lightly with honey and sprinkle with ground ginger if desired.
3. Arrange the rings in a single layer in the air fryer basket.
4. Air fry for 5 minutes, flipping halfway, until lightly caramelized.
5. Serve warm as a refreshing treat or with a dollop of Greek yogurt.

TIPS & MODIFICATIONS:
- Substitute fresh pineapple with canned (low-sodium) if fresh is unavailable.
- Drizzle with coconut cream for a tropical feel.
- Store leftovers in the fridge for up to 1 day; reheat briefly in the air fryer before serving.

NUTRITIONAL BREAKDOWN:
Sugar: 6g (from pineapple), **Fiber**: 1g, **Potassium**: 90mg, **Sodium**: 0mg

Air Fryer Zucchini Fries

Cooking Time: 10 minutes
Preparation Time: 10 minutes
Serving Size: 1/2 cup

INGREDIENT LIST:
- 1 medium zucchini, sliced into thin strips
- 1/4 cup panko breadcrumbs (low-sodium)
- 1/4 tsp garlic powder
- 1/4 tsp paprika
- 1 egg white, beaten

INSTRUCTIONS:
1. Preheat the air fryer to 375°F (190°C).
2. In a bowl, mix the breadcrumbs, garlic powder, and paprika.
3. Dip each zucchini strip in egg white, then coat with the breadcrumb mixture.

4. Place zucchini strips in a single layer in the air fryer basket.
5. Air fry for 8-10 minutes, turning halfway, until crispy and golden.

TIPS & MODIFICATIONS:
- Try yellow squash for a similar flavor.
- Serve with low-sodium marinara for dipping.

NUTRITIONAL BREAKDOWN:
Fiber: 2g, *Potassium*: 180mg, *Sodium*: 10mg

Air Fryer Cauliflower Tots

Cooking Time: 15 minutes
Preparation Time: 10 minutes
Serving Size: 6 tots

INGREDIENT LIST:
- 1 cup cauliflower florets, steamed and mashed
- 1/4 cup panko breadcrumbs (low-sodium)
- 1 egg white
- 1/4 tsp garlic powder

INSTRUCTIONS:
1. Preheat the air fryer to 375°F (190°C).
2. Mix cauliflower, breadcrumbs, egg white, and garlic powder until combined.
3. Form mixture into small tots and place in the air fryer.
4. Air fry for 12-15 minutes until golden and crispy.

NUTRITIONAL BREAKDOWN:
Fiber: 3g, *Potassium*: 110mg, *Sodium*: 20mg

Air Fryer Green Bean Fries

Cooking Time: 8 minutes
Preparation Time: 5 minutes
Serving Size: 1/2 cup

INGREDIENT LIST:
- 1/2 lb fresh green beans, trimmed
- 1 tbsp olive oil
- 1/4 tsp garlic powder

INSTRUCTIONS:
1. Preheat air fryer to 375°F (190°C).
2. Toss green beans with olive oil and garlic powder.
3. Place in the air fryer and cook for 6-8 minutes until crisp.

TIPS & MODIFICATIONS:
- Substitute olive oil with avocado oil for variety.
- Serve with a lemon wedge for extra flavor.

NUTRITIONAL BREAKDOWN:
Fiber: 2g, *Potassium*: 100mg, *Sodium*: 0mg

Air Fryer Cinnamon Pear Chips

Cooking Time: 12 minutes
Preparation Time: 3 minutes
Serving Size: 1/2 cup

INGREDIENT LIST:
- 1 pear, thinly sliced
- 1/2 tsp cinnamon

INSTRUCTIONS:
1. Preheat air fryer to 300°F (150°C).
2. Sprinkle cinnamon on pear slices.
3. Place in the air fryer and cook for 10-12 minutes until crisp, turning halfway.

TIPS & MODIFICATIONS:
Store leftovers in an airtight container.
Substitute pears with apples if desired.

NUTRITIONAL BREAKDOWN:
Sugar: 5g, *Fiber*: 2g, *Potassium*: 90mg

Air Fryer Veggie Nuggets

Cooking Time: 10 minutes
Preparation Time: 10 minutes
Serving Size: 5 nuggets

INGREDIENT LIST:
- 1/2 cup steamed carrots, mashed
- 1/2 cup breadcrumbs (low-sodium)

- 1/4 cup grated zucchini
- 1 egg white

INSTRUCTIONS:
1. Preheat air fryer to 375°F (190°C).
2. mix ingredients and shape into nuggets.
3. Air fry for 8-10 minutes, flipping halfway, until crispy.

TIPS & MODIFICATIONS:
- Serve with low-sodium ketchup.
- Swap breadcrumbs with almond flour for added texture.

NUTRITIONAL BREAKDOWN:
Fiber: 2g, *Potassium*: 120mg

Air Fryer Spiced Peaches

Cooking Time: 5 minutes
Preparation Time: 3 minutes
Serving Size: 1/2 peach

INGREDIENT LIST:
- 1 peach, halved
- 1/4 tsp cinnamon

INSTRUCTIONS:
1. Preheat air fryer to 375°F (190°C).
2. Sprinkle cinnamon on peach halves.
3. Air fry for 5 minutes until tender.

TIPS & MODIFICATIONS:
- Add a small dollop of Greek yogurt.
- Substitute peaches with apples for variety.

NUTRITIONAL BREAKDOWN:
Fiber: 1g, *Potassium*: 150mg

Air Fryer Strawberry Bites

Cooking Time: 5 minutes
Preparation Time: 2 minutes
Serving Size: 1/2 cup

INGREDIENT LIST:
- 1/2 cup fresh strawberries, halved

INSTRUCTIONS:
1. Preheat air fryer to 375°F (190°C).
2. Place strawberries in the air fryer basket.
3. Air fry for 5 minutes until softened.

TIPS & MODIFICATIONS:
- Top with unsweetened whipped cream if desired.
- Add a sprinkle of cinnamon for extra flavor.

NUTRITIONAL BREAKDOWN:
Fiber: 2g, *Potassium*: 100mg

Air Fryer Cinnamon Carrot Sticks

Cooking Time: 10 minutes
Preparation Time: 5 minutes
Serving Size: 1/2 cup

INGREDIENT LIST:
- 1 large carrot, cut into sticks
- 1/4 tsp cinnamon

INSTRUCTIONS:
1. Preheat air fryer to 375°F (190°C).
2. Toss carrot sticks with cinnamon.
3. Air fry for 8-10 minutes, shaking halfway.

TIPS & MODIFICATIONS:
- Serve warm with a drizzle of honey.
- Swap carrots for parsnips if desired.

NUTRITIONAL BREAKDOWN:
Fiber: 2g, *Potassium*: 150mg

Air Fryer Pear & Cranberry Crisp

Cooking Time: 15 minutes
Preparation Time: 5 minutes
Serving Size: 1/2 cup

INGREDIENT LIST:
- 1 pear, chopped
- 1 tbsp dried cranberries (unsweetened)
- 1 tbsp almond flour

INSTRUCTIONS:
1. Preheat air fryer to 350°F (175°C).
2. mix all ingredients and place in an air fryer-safe dish.
3. Air fry for 12-15 minutes until warm and slightly bubbly.

TIPS & MODIFICATIONS:
- Substitute cranberries with blueberries.
- Serve with a small spoonful of Greek yogurt.

NUTRITIONAL BREAKDOWN:
Fiber: 3g, **Potassium**: 100mg

Air Fryer Pumpkin Chips

Cooking Time: 10 minutes
Preparation Time: 3 minutes
Serving Size: 1/2 cup

INGREDIENT LIST:
- 1 cup pumpkin, thinly sliced
- 1/4 tsp cinnamon

INSTRUCTIONS:
1. Preheat air fryer to 300°F (150°C).
2. Place pumpkin slices in air fryer and cook for 8-10 minutes.

TIPS & MODIFICATIONS:
Try adding a sprinkle of nutmeg.
Store in an airtight container for up to 2 days.

NUTRITIONAL BREAKDOWN:
Fiber: 2g, **Potassium**: 100mg

Air Fryer Apple Pie Bites

Cooking Time: 5 minutes
Preparation Time: 3 minutes
Serving Size: 2 bites

INGREDIENT LIST:
- 1 apple, chopped
- 1/4 tsp cinnamon

INSTRUCTIONS:
1. Preheat air fryer to 375°F (190°C).
2. Toss apple chunks with cinnamon.
3. Air fry for 5 minutes until softened.

TIPS & MODIFICATIONS:
Serve warm with a spoonful of plain Greek yogurt

NUTRITIONAL BREAKDOWN:
Fiber: 2g, **Potassium**: 110mg

Chapter 12: MEAL PLANNING AND BATCH COOKING FOR KIDNEY HEALTH

Sample Meal Plans: 60-Day Kidney-Friendly Meal Plan

Day 1
- **Breakfast:** Berry Bliss Smoothie (*200 Kcal*)
- **Snack:** Cucumber Avocado Bites (*120 Kcal*)
- **Lunch:** Crisp Cucumber & Herb Salad with Lemon Vinaigrette (*180 Kcal*)
- **Dinner:** Zesty Lemon Herb Chicken with Roasted Veggies (*320 Kcal*)

Day 2
- **Breakfast:** Pumpkin Spice Oatmeal (*240 Kcal*)
- **Snack:** Blueberry Oat Energy Bites (*130 Kcal*)
- **Lunch:** Herbed Vegetable & Barley Stew (*230 Kcal*)
- **Dinner:** Garlic Butter Shrimp and Asparagus Sheet Pan (*350 Kcal*)

Day 3
- **Breakfast:** Coconut Almond Chia Pudding (*220 Kcal*)
- **Snack:** Spiced Roasted Sweet Potato Cubes (*140 Kcal*)
- **Lunch:** Brown Rice & Broccoli Bowl with Miso Dressing (*260 Kcal*)
- **Dinner:** Herb-Crusted Tilapia with Roasted Carrots & Peppers (*340 Kcal*)

Day 4
- **Breakfast:** Egg White Veggie Omelette (*180 Kcal*)
- **Snack:** Kale Chips with Sea Salt (*110 Kcal*)
- **Lunch:** Turkey Lettuce Wraps (*250 Kcal*)
- **Dinner:** Quinoa-Stuffed Bell Peppers with

Avocado Dressing (*300 Kcal*)

Day 5
- **Breakfast:** Oatmeal with Apples and Cinnamon (*230 Kcal*)
- **Snack:** Lemon-Parsley Cauliflower Rice (*120 Kcal*)
- **Lunch:** Hummus & Veggie Wrap with Crunchy Cabbage (*200 Kcal*)
- **Dinner:** Baked Cod with Garlic and Fresh Lemon (*320 Kcal*)

Day 6
- **Breakfast:** Green Goodness Smoothie (*210 Kcal*)
- **Snack:** Cinnamon Spiced Apple Slices (*100 Kcal*)
- **Lunch:** Lentil and Carrot Soup (*230 Kcal*)
- **Dinner:** Sweet Potato and Lentil Shepherd's Pie (*330 Kcal*)

Day 7
- **Breakfast:** Heart-Healthy Oatmeal (*240 Kcal*)
- **Snack:** Roasted Garlic Cauliflower Bites (*120 Kcal*)
- **Lunch:** Cilantro Lime Farro & Veggie Bowl (*260 Kcal*)
- **Dinner:** Grilled Salmon with Avocado Salsa (*350 Kcal*)

Day 8
- **Breakfast:** Apple Cinnamon Delight Smoothie (*220 Kcal*)
- **Snack:** Zesty Herb Cottage Cheese Spread (*120 Kcal*)
- **Lunch:** Avocado & Cabbage Slaw with Fresh Herbs (*250 Kcal*)
- **Dinner:** One-Pan Mediterranean Salmon with Olives & Veggies (*360 Kcal*)

Day 9
- **Breakfast:** Coconut Oats Delight (*240 Kcal*)
- **Snack:** Lemon and Garlic Avocado Dip with Veggie Sticks (*130 Kcal*)
- **Lunch:** No-Salt Minestrone Soup (*230 Kcal*)
- **Dinner:** Sweet Potato and Lentil Shepherd's Pie (*330 Kcal*)

Day 10
- **Breakfast:** Chia Flax Fiber Porridge (*220 Kcal*)

- **Snack:** Cinnamon Spiced Apple Slices (*100 Kcal*)
- **Lunch:** Turkey & Zucchini Wrap with Lemon Aioli (*270 Kcal*)
- **Dinner:** Herb-Marinated Grilled Chicken with Spinach and Tomatoes (*320 Kcal*)

Day 11
- **Breakfast:** Avocado and Egg Breakfast Wrap (*240 Kcal*)
- **Snack:** Air Fryer Zucchini Fries (*120 Kcal*)
- **Lunch:** Lentil and Carrot Soup (*230 Kcal*)
- **Dinner:** Stuffed Acorn Squash with Brown Rice and Cranberries (*350 Kcal*)

Day 12
- **Breakfast:** Peach and Yogurt Parfait (*200 Kcal*)
- **Snack:** Homemade Guacamole with Veggie Sticks (*140 Kcal*)
- **Lunch:** Berry & Spinach Salad with Poppy Seed Dressing (*260 Kcal*)
- **Dinner:** Baked Chicken Thighs with Sweet Potatoes & Green Beans (*360 Kcal*)

Day 13
- **Breakfast:** Berry Breakfast Quinoa Bowl (*230 Kcal*)
- **Snack:** Roasted Garlic Cauliflower Bites (*120 Kcal*)
- **Lunch:** Cilantro Lime Farro & Veggie Bowl (*250 Kcal*)
- **Dinner:** Baked Cod with Garlic and Fresh Lemon (*340 Kcal*)

Day 14
- **Breakfast:** Tofu Scramble with Bell Peppers (*210 Kcal*)
- **Snack:** Blueberry Lemon Sorbet (*140 Kcal*)
- **Lunch:** Herbed Chicken & Cucumber Sandwich (*280 Kcal*)
- **Dinner:** Grilled Salmon with Asparagus (*330 Kcal*)

Day 15
- **Breakfast:** Pumpkin Spice Oatmeal (*230 Kcal*)
- **Snack:** Air Fryer Cinnamon Apple Chips (*110 Kcal*)
- **Lunch:** Herbed Vegetable & Barley Stew (*250 Kcal*)

- **Dinner:** Citrus-Glazed Trout with Roasted Asparagus (*350 Kcal*)

Day 16
- **Breakfast:** Coconut Almond Chia Pudding (*220 Kcal*)
- **Snack:** Baked Cinnamon Squash Fries (*130 Kcal*)
- **Lunch:** Turkey Lettuce Wraps (*250 Kcal*)
- **Dinner:** Lentil and Spinach Pasta in a Light Tomato Sauce (*320 Kcal*)

Day 17
- **Breakfast:** Sweet Potato and Spinach Breakfast Bowl (*250 Kcal*)
- **Snack:** Cinnamon Pear Compote with Agave (*130 Kcal*)
- **Lunch:** Simple Sweet Potato & Leek Soup (*240 Kcal*)
- **Dinner:** Salmon and Veggie Foil Packets (*360 Kcal*)

Day 18
- **Breakfast:** Green Goodness Smoothie (*210 Kcal*)
- **Snack:** Crispy Zucchini Chips with Fresh Dill (*110 Kcal*)
- **Lunch:** Egg White Salad Wrap with Fresh Dill (*260 Kcal*)
- **Dinner:** Chickpea and Zucchini Pasta with Pesto Sauce (*340 Kcal*)

Day 19
- **Breakfast:** Egg White Veggie Omelette (*200 Kcal*)
- **Snack:** Berry Coconut Parfait (*120 Kcal*)
- **Lunch:** Brown Rice & Broccoli Bowl with Miso Dressing (*260 Kcal*)
- **Dinner:** Sweet Potato and Lentil Shepherd's Pie (*330 Kcal*)

Day 20
- **Breakfast:** Heart-Healthy Oatmeal (*240 Kcal*)
- **Snack:** Kale Chips with Sea Salt (*110 Kcal*)
- **Lunch:** Lentil and Carrot Soup (*230 Kcal*)
- **Dinner:** Herb-Crusted Tilapia with Roasted Carrots & Peppers (*350 Kcal*)

Day 21
- **Breakfast:** Strawberry Almond Dream Smoothie (*210 Kcal*)

- **Snack:** Creamy White Bean and Basil Dip with Veggies (*130 Kcal*)
- **Lunch:** Roasted Red Pepper & Avocado Sandwich (*250 Kcal*)
- **Dinner:** Stuffed Bell Peppers with Quinoa and Turkey (*330 Kcal*)

Day 22
- **Breakfast:** Cinnamon Apple Quinoa Porridge (*230 Kcal*)
- **Snack:** Roasted Garlic Cauliflower Bites (*120 Kcal*)
- **Lunch:** Zucchini Noodles with Pesto (*260 Kcal*)
- **Dinner:** Quinoa-Stuffed Bell Peppers with Avocado Dressing (*340 Kcal*)

Day 23
- **Breakfast:** Berry Bliss Smoothie (*210 Kcal*)
- **Snack:** Spiced Roasted Sweet Potato Cubes (*120 Kcal*)
- **Lunch:** Grilled Chicken and Veggie Salad (*280 Kcal*)
- **Dinner:** Pan-Seared Chicken Breast with Roasted Brussels Sprouts (*350 Kcal*)

Day 24
- **Breakfast:** Low-Sodium Sweet Potato Hash (*230 Kcal*)
- **Snack:** Blueberry Oat Energy Bites (*130 Kcal*)
- **Lunch:** Wild Rice & Apple Salad with Maple Dressing (*250 Kcal*)
- **Dinner:** Baked Cod with Garlic and Fresh Lemon (*340 Kcal*)

Day 25
- **Breakfast:** Coconut Oats Delight (*240 Kcal*)
- **Snack:** Lemon-Parsley Cauliflower Rice (*120 Kcal*)
- **Lunch:** Lentil and Carrot Soup (*230 Kcal*)
- **Dinner:** Sweet Potato and Lentil Shepherd's Pie (*330 Kcal*)

Day 26
- **Breakfast:** Chia Flax Fiber Porridge (*220 Kcal*)
- **Snack:** Cucumber Avocado Bites (*110 Kcal*)
- **Lunch:** Hummus & Veggie Wrap with Crunchy Cabbage (*240 Kcal*)
- **Dinner:** Easy Herb-Crusted Tilapia with Roasted Carrots & Peppers (*350 Kcal*)

Day 27
- **Breakfast:** Oatmeal with Apples and Cinnamon (*230 Kcal*)
- **Snack:** Air Fryer Pumpkin Chips (*120 Kcal*)
- **Lunch:** Low-Potassium Greek Chickpea Salad (*250 Kcal*)
- **Dinner:** Grilled Salmon with Avocado Salsa (*330 Kcal*)

Day 28
- **Breakfast:** Peach and Yogurt Parfait (*210 Kcal*)
- **Snack:** Cinnamon Pear Chips (*110 Kcal*)
- **Lunch:** Warm Quinoa Bowl with Spinach & Roasted Peppers (*270 Kcal*)
- **Dinner:** Zesty Lemon Herb Chicken with Roasted Veggies (*360 Kcal*)

Day 29
- **Breakfast:** Tofu Scramble with Bell Peppers (*220 Kcal*)
- **Snack:** Roasted Carrot and Zucchini Medley (*120 Kcal*)
- **Lunch:** Turkey & Zucchini Wrap with Lemon Aioli (*250 Kcal*)
- **Dinner:** Chickpea & Spinach Stew with Turmeric and Cumin (*330 Kcal*)

Day 30
- **Breakfast:** Sweet Potato and Spinach Breakfast Bowl (*250 Kcal*)
- **Snack:** Cinnamon Apple Muffins with Oats (*130 Kcal*)
- **Lunch:** Colorful Quinoa & Veggie Medley (*260 Kcal*)
- **Dinner:** Garlic Butter Shrimp and Asparagus Sheet Pan (*340 Kcal*)

Day 31
- **Breakfast:** Green Goodness Smoothie (*210 Kcal*)
- **Snack:** Creamy White Bean and Basil Dip with Veggies (*130 Kcal*)
- **Lunch:** Egg White Salad Wrap with Fresh Dill (*240 Kcal*)
- **Dinner:** Herb-Marinated Grilled Chicken with Spinach and Tomatoes (*320 Kcal*)

Day 32
- **Breakfast:** Berry Breakfast Quinoa Bowl (*230 Kcal*)
- **Snack:** Kale Chips with Sea Salt (*110 Kcal*)

- **Lunch:** Avocado & Cabbage Slaw with Fresh Herbs (*250 Kcal*)
- **Dinner:** Citrus-Glazed Trout with Roasted Asparagus (*350 Kcal*)

Day 33
- **Breakfast:** Cinnamon Apple Quinoa Porridge (*230 Kcal*)
- **Snack:** Crispy Zucchini Chips with Fresh Dill (*120 Kcal*)
- **Lunch:** Roasted Red Pepper & Avocado Sandwich (*250 Kcal*)
- **Dinner:** Lentil and Spinach Pasta in a Light Tomato Sauce (*330 Kcal*)

Day 34
- **Breakfast:** Strawberry Almond Dream Smoothie (*210 Kcal*)
- **Snack:** Homemade Guacamole with Veggie Sticks (*140 Kcal*)
- **Lunch:** Herbed Vegetable & Barley Stew (*260 Kcal*)
- **Dinner:** Sweet Potato and Lentil Shepherd's Pie (*330 Kcal*)

Day 35
- **Breakfast:** Heart-Healthy Oatmeal (*240 Kcal*)
- **Snack:** Cinnamon Spiced Apple Slices (*110 Kcal*)
- **Lunch:** Hummus & Veggie Wrap with Crunchy Cabbage (*240 Kcal*)
- **Dinner:** Stuffed Bell Peppers with Quinoa and Turkey (*340 Kcal*)

Day 36
- **Breakfast:** Egg White Veggie Omelette (*220 Kcal*)
- **Snack:** Apple and Almond Butter Slices (*130 Kcal*)
- **Lunch:** Brown Rice & Broccoli Bowl with Miso Dressing (*260 Kcal*)
- **Dinner:** Grilled Salmon with Asparagus (*330 Kcal*)

Day 37
- **Breakfast:** Avocado and Egg Breakfast Wrap (*240 Kcal*)
- **Snack:** Low-Sodium Greek Yogurt Herb Dip (*110 Kcal*)
- **Lunch:** Lentil and Carrot Soup (*230 Kcal*)
- **Dinner:** One-Pan Mediterranean Salmon with Olives & Veggies (*350 Kcal*)

Day 38
- **Breakfast:** Pumpkin Spice Oatmeal (*230 Kcal*)
- **Snack:** Lemon and Garlic Avocado Dip (*120 Kcal*)
- **Lunch:** Turkey Lettuce Wraps (*240 Kcal*)
- **Dinner:** Herb-Crusted Tilapia with Roasted Veggies (*340 Kcal*)

Day 39
- **Breakfast:** Coconut Almond Chia Pudding (*210 Kcal*)
- **Snack:** Baked Cinnamon Squash Fries (*110 Kcal*)
- **Lunch:** Wild Rice & Apple Salad with Maple Dressing (*250 Kcal*)
- **Dinner:** Sweet Potato and Lentil Shepherd's Pie (*330 Kcal*)

Day 40
- **Breakfast:** Poached Eggs on Whole Wheat Toast (*220 Kcal*)
- **Snack:** Kale Chips with Sea Salt (*120 Kcal*)
- **Lunch:** Crisp Cucumber & Herb Salad with Lemon Vinaigrette (*240 Kcal*)
- **Dinner:** Garlic Butter Shrimp and Asparagus Sheet Pan (*340 Kcal*)

Day 41
- **Breakfast:** Chia Flax Fiber Porridge (*220 Kcal*)
- **Snack:** Cinnamon Apple Muffins with Oats (*130 Kcal*)
- **Lunch:** Hummus & Veggie Wrap with Crunchy Cabbage (*240 Kcal*)
- **Dinner:** Baked Cod with Garlic and Fresh Lemon (*340 Kcal*)

Day 42
- **Breakfast:** Tropical Sunrise Smoothie (*210 Kcal*)
- **Snack:** Air Fryer Cinnamon Apple Chips (*110 Kcal*)
- **Lunch:** Cilantro Lime Farro & Veggie Bowl (*250 Kcal*)
- **Dinner:** Herb-Marinated Grilled Chicken with Spinach and Tomatoes (*320 Kcal*)

Day 43
- **Breakfast:** Coconut Oats Delight (*230 Kcal*)
- **Snack:** Blueberry Oat Energy Bites (*120 Kcal*)
- **Lunch:** Avocado & Cabbage Slaw with Fresh Herbs (*250 Kcal*)

- **Dinner:** Citrus-Glazed Trout with Roasted Asparagus (*350 Kcal*)

Day 44
- **Breakfast:** Berry Bliss Smoothie (*210 Kcal*)
- **Snack:** Zesty Herb Cottage Cheese Spread with Veggies (*130 Kcal*)
- **Lunch:** Warm Quinoa Bowl with Spinach & Roasted Peppers (*260 Kcal*)
- **Dinner:** Sweet Potato and Lentil Shepherd's Pie (*330 Kcal*)

Day 45
- **Breakfast:** Green Goodness Smoothie (*210 Kcal*)
- **Snack:** Spiced Roasted Sweet Potato Cubes (*120 Kcal*)
- **Lunch:** No-Salt Minestrone Soup (*230 Kcal*)
- **Dinner:** Pan-Seared Chicken Breast with Roasted Brussels Sprouts (*340 Kcal*)

Day 46
- **Breakfast:** Heart-Healthy Oatmeal (*240 Kcal*)
- **Snack:** Crispy Zucchini Chips with Fresh Dill (*120 Kcal*)
- **Lunch:** Lentil and Carrot Soup (*230 Kcal*)
- **Dinner:** Herb-Crusted Tilapia with Roasted Veggies (*350 Kcal*)

Day 47
- **Breakfast:** Chia Flax Fiber Porridge (*220 Kcal*)
- **Snack:** Apple and Almond Butter Slices (*130 Kcal*)
- **Lunch:** Grilled Chicken and Veggie Salad (*280 Kcal*)
- **Dinner:** Baked Chicken Thighs with Sweet Potatoes & Green Beans (*340 Kcal*)

Day 48
- **Breakfast:** Pumpkin Spice Oatmeal (*230 Kcal*)
- **Snack:** Creamy White Bean and Basil Dip with Veggies (*130 Kcal*)
- **Lunch:** Zucchini Noodles with Pesto (*260 Kcal*)
- **Dinner:** Garlic Butter Shrimp and Asparagus Sheet Pan (*340 Kcal*)

Day 49
- **Breakfast:** Berry Quinoa Breakfast Bowl (*240 Kcal*)

- **Snack:** Kale Chips with Sea Salt (*110 Kcal*)
- **Lunch:** Avocado & Cabbage Slaw with Fresh Herbs (*250 Kcal*)
- **Dinner:** Sweet Potato and Lentil Shepherd's Pie (*330 Kcal*)

Day 50
- **Breakfast:** Tropical Sunrise Smoothie (*210 Kcal*)
- **Snack:** Baked Cinnamon Squash Fries (*120 Kcal*)
- **Lunch:** Wild Rice & Apple Salad with Maple Dressing (*250 Kcal*)
- **Dinner:** Herb-Marinated Grilled Chicken with Spinach and Tomatoes (*320 Kcal*)

Day 51
- **Breakfast:** Cinnamon Apple Quinoa Porridge (*230 Kcal*)
- **Snack:** Zesty Apple and Cabbage Slaw (*130 Kcal*)
- **Lunch:** Crisp Cucumber & Herb Salad with Lemon Vinaigrette (*240 Kcal*)
- **Dinner:** Pan-Seared Chicken Breast with Roasted Brussels Sprouts (*340 Kcal*)

Day 52
- **Breakfast:** Sweet Potato and Spinach Breakfast Bowl (*250 Kcal*)
- **Snack:** Spiced Roasted Sweet Potato Cubes (*120 Kcal*)
- **Lunch:** Lentil and Carrot Soup (*230 Kcal*)
- **Dinner:** Grilled Salmon with Asparagus (*330 Kcal*)

Day 53
- **Breakfast:** Avocado and Egg Breakfast Wrap (*240 Kcal*)
- **Snack:** Apple and Almond Butter Slices (*130 Kcal*)
- **Lunch:** No-Salt Minestrone Soup (*230 Kcal*)
- **Dinner:** Citrus-Glazed Trout with Roasted Asparagus (*350 Kcal*)

Day 54
- **Breakfast:** Green Goodness Smoothie (*210 Kcal*)
- **Snack:** Cinnamon Apple Muffins with Oats (*130 Kcal*)
- **Lunch:** Grilled Chicken and Veggie Salad (*280 Kcal*)

- **Dinner:** Lentil and Spinach Pasta in a Light Tomato Sauce (*330 Kcal*)

Day 55
- **Breakfast:** Chia Flax Fiber Porridge (*220 Kcal*)
- **Snack:** Air Fryer Cinnamon Apple Chips (*110 Kcal*)
- **Lunch:** Hummus & Veggie Wrap with Crunchy Cabbage (*240 Kcal*)
- **Dinner:** Herb-Crusted Tilapia with Roasted Veggies (*350 Kcal*)

Day 56
- **Breakfast:** Heart-Healthy Oatmeal (*240 Kcal*)
- **Snack:** Kale Chips with Sea Salt (*110 Kcal*)
- **Lunch:** Lentil and Carrot Soup (*230 Kcal*)
- **Dinner:** Sweet Potato and Lentil Shepherd's Pie (*330 Kcal*)

Day 57
- **Breakfast:** Berry Bliss Smoothie (*210 Kcal*)
- **Snack:** Lemon-Parsley Cauliflower Rice (*120 Kcal*)
- **Lunch:** Zucchini Noodles with Pesto (*260 Kcal*)
- **Dinner:** Herb-Marinated Grilled Chicken with Spinach and Tomatoes (*320 Kcal*)

Day 58
- **Breakfast:** Poached Eggs on Whole Wheat Toast (*220 Kcal*)
- **Snack:** Blueberry Oat Energy Bites (*130 Kcal*)
- **Lunch:** Warm Quinoa Bowl with Spinach & Roasted Peppers (*270 Kcal*)
- **Dinner:** Citrus-Glazed Trout with Roasted Asparagus (*350 Kcal*)

Day 59
- **Breakfast:** Low-Sodium Sweet Potato Hash (*230 Kcal*)
- **Snack:** Zesty Herb Cottage Cheese Spread with Veggies (*130 Kcal*)
- **Lunch:** Hummus & Veggie Wrap with Crunchy Cabbage (*240 Kcal*)
- **Dinner:** Garlic Butter Shrimp and Asparagus Sheet Pan (*340 Kcal*)

Day 60
- **Breakfast:** Strawberry Almond Dream Smoothie (*210 Kcal*)

- **Snack:** Baked Cinnamon Squash Fries (*120 Kcal*)
- **Lunch:** Lentil and Carrot Soup (*230 Kcal*)
- **Dinner:** Sweet Potato and Lentil Shepherd's Pie (*330 Kcal*)

60-Day Shopping List for Kidney Health

Fresh Produce
- **Vegetables**
    - Asparagus (fresh) – 6-8 bundles
    - Zucchini – 12
    - Cauliflower – 6 heads
    - Sweet potatoes – 15 medium
    - Broccoli – 4 heads
    - Brussels sprouts – 6 cups
    - Carrots – 24 medium
    - Green beans – 8 cups
    - Spinach (fresh) – 20 cups
    - Kale – 12 cups
    - Bell peppers (red, green, yellow) – 20
    - Tomatoes – 16
    - Cucumbers – 14
    - Avocados – 15
    - Cabbage (red/green) – 2 small heads
    - Butternut squash – 4 small
    - Leeks – 4 medium
    - Onions (yellow/red) – 12
    - Garlic – 10 bulbs
    - Fresh herbs (parsley, cilantro, basil, rosemary, thyme, dill) – 2 bundles of each
- **Fruits**
    - Apples (variety) – 20
    - Bananas – 16
    - Strawberries (fresh or frozen) – 6 lbs
    - Blueberries (fresh or frozen) – 5 lbs

- Mangoes – 10
- Pineapple – 4
- Kiwi – 6
- Peaches – 6
- Pears – 6
- Watermelon – 1 medium
- Lemons – 12
- Limes – 8
- Cranberries (fresh or unsweetened dried) – 2 cups

Proteins
- **Eggs**
  - Egg whites (liquid cartons or fresh eggs) – 6 dozen
- **Meat/Poultry**
  - Skinless chicken breasts – 20 lbs
  - Skinless chicken thighs – 12 lbs
  - Turkey breast – 4 lbs
- **Seafood**
  - Salmon (fresh or frozen) – 10 lbs
  - Cod – 6 lbs
  - Tilapia – 6 lbs
  - Shrimp (medium, peeled, deveined) – 8 lbs
  - Trout – 6 lbs
- **Plant-Based Proteins**
  - Tofu (firm) – 6 blocks
  - Lentils (dried or canned) – 8 cups
  - Chickpeas (canned or dried) – 10 cups
  - Black beans (canned or dried) – 6 cups
  - White beans (canned or dried) – 6 cups

Grains and Starches
- Quinoa (regular or tricolor) – 12 cups
- Brown rice – 8 cups
- Wild rice – 6 cups
- Farro – 6 cups
- Barley – 6 cups
- Whole wheat pasta – 8 cups
- Whole wheat bread (low-sodium) – 6 loaves
- Whole wheat tortillas – 4 packs

- Rolled oats – 12 cups

Dairy & Dairy Alternatives
- Unsweetened almond milk – 6 cartons (1 liter each)
- Low-sodium cottage cheese – 4 tubs (500g each)
- Plain Greek yogurt (low-sodium) – 6 tubs (500g each)

Pantry Staples
- **Canned/Packaged Goods**
  - No-salt-added vegetable broth – 8 cartons
  - No-salt-added diced tomatoes – 8 cans
  - Unsweetened applesauce – 6 cups
- **Nuts and Seeds**
  - Chia seeds – 2 cups
  - Flaxseeds (ground) – 2 cups
  - Almonds (unsalted) – 4 cups
  - Walnuts (unsalted) – 3 cups
- **Oils and Vinegars**
  - Olive oil – 2 liters
  - Avocado oil – 1 liter
  - Balsamic vinegar – 2 cups
  - Apple cider vinegar – 2 cups
- **Herbs and Spices**
  - Cinnamon
  - Nutmeg
  - Cumin
  - Turmeric
  - Paprika (sweet or smoked)
  - Garlic powder
  - Onion powder
  - Black pepper
  - Dried basil
  - Dried oregano

Snacks and Treats Ingredients
- o Dried thyme
- Unsweetened cocoa powder – 2 cups
- Almond flour – 6 cups
- Honey – 3 cups
- Maple syrup (pure) – 2 cups
- Coconut flakes (unsweetened) – 2 cups

Beverages and Hydration
- Herbal teas (chamomile, ginger, peppermint) – 4 boxes
- Fresh ginger – 4 knobs
- Fresh mint – 4 bundles
- Sparkling water (unsweetened) – Optional

Air Fryer Recipes Staples
- Whole wheat breadcrumbs – 4 cups
- Cooking spray (low-sodium) – 1 bottle

CKD Stage Nutritional Guide

Below is a visual chart to guide the you in understanding the recommended intake of nutrients (protein, potassium, sodium, and fluids) at each CKD stage. This will you help tailor the meal plans according to your progression of CKD and individual dietary needs.

CKD Stage	Protein	Potassium	Sodium	Fluids
Stage 1	Moderate (0.8–1.0g/kg)	Moderate (2,000–3,000 mg)	≤ 2,300 mg	No restriction
Stage 2	Moderate (0.6–0.8g/kg)	Moderate (2,000–3,000 mg)	≤ 2,300 mg	No restriction

Stage 3	Reduced (0.6g/kg)	Low (1,500–2,000 mg)	≤ 1,500 mg	Fluid restriction based on individual needs
Stage 4	Lower (0.6g/kg)	Low (1,000–1,500 mg)	≤ 1,500 mg	Fluid restriction based on individual needs
Stage 5	Very Low (0.4g/kg)	Very Low (800–1,000 mg)	≤ 1,000 mg	Strict fluid restriction (usually 500–700 ml/day)

Guidelines for Adjusting the Meal Plan by CKD Stages

For individuals at different stages of chronic kidney disease (CKD), this meal plan offers flexibility with modifications to meet specific dietary needs. Adjustments focus on protein, potassium, sodium, and fluid intake to accommodate each stage of CKD, helping to maintain optimal kidney function while enjoying a variety of nutritious meals.

Stage 1–2: Early CKD (Mild)

- **Protein**: Moderate protein intake is suitable, so meals with lean protein sources (such as chicken or tofu) can be enjoyed without adjustments.

- **Potassium**: Stick to a moderate intake. Most recipes in this meal plan are naturally lower in high-potassium ingredients, but monitor portion sizes for foods like bananas and avocado.

- **Sodium**: Aim for < 2,300 mg daily. The plan's low-sodium approach fits well, so minimal adjustments are needed.

- **Fluids**: No specific restriction, but staying hydrated is beneficial for overall kidney health.

Stage 3: Moderate CKD

- **Protein**: Start reducing protein portions slightly. For dishes like chickpea salads or lentil stews, use smaller portions, focusing on high-quality, plant-based proteins in moderate amounts.
- **Potassium**: Emphasize low-potassium vegetables and fruits. Reduce portions of higher-potassium ingredients (e.g., avocados, potatoes) and substitute with lower-potassium options (e.g., bell peppers, apples).
- **Sodium**: Limit intake to < 1,500 mg daily. Avoid adding any extra salt to recipes, and use low-sodium seasonings.
- **Fluids**: No specific limit yet, but avoid excess fluid intake if directed by a healthcare provider.

Stage 4: Advanced CKD

- **Protein**: Further reduce protein to a low-moderate intake, especially from animal sources. In recipes with lentils, beans, or chicken, consider using half the recommended portion and bulking up meals with additional low-potassium vegetables.
- **Potassium**: Stick to low-potassium produce as much as possible. Avoid high-potassium items like tomatoes, bananas, and oranges. Substitute with options like cauliflower, cucumber, and strawberries where possible.

- **Sodium**: Continue with a strict low-sodium approach, aiming for < 1,500 mg. Avoid pre-seasoned or pre-packaged foods unless labeled "low sodium."
- **Fluids**: Begin to moderate fluid intake if advised by a healthcare provider, as the kidneys may have more difficulty managing fluid balance.

Stage 5: End-Stage CKD (Severe)

- **Protein**: Protein intake should be very low, typically focused on high-quality sources like eggs in very limited quantities. Consider vegetarian days and use plant-based proteins sparingly.
- **Potassium**: Choose low-potassium foods exclusively. Completely avoid higher-potassium vegetables like spinach and potatoes, and select low-potassium alternatives such as lettuce, bell peppers, and blueberries.
- **Sodium**: Keep sodium intake extremely low, ideally < 1,000 mg daily. Use only fresh ingredients and avoid any processed or canned foods unless labeled very low in sodium.
- **Fluids**: Restrict fluids according to medical guidance, especially if experiencing swelling or other symptoms of fluid retention. Be mindful of foods that contain high water content (like soups or smoothies).

Meal Adjustment Tips for All Stages

- **Portion Control**: Adjust portion sizes based on stage-specific protein, potassium, and sodium needs. For example, reduce portion sizes of protein-rich foods like meat or beans in higher CKD stages.

- **Vegetable Selection**: Use lower-potassium vegetables (e.g., green beans, cauliflower) as staple ingredients, especially for advanced CKD stages. Replace high-potassium vegetables in recipes with these options when necessary.

- **Recipe Modifications**: Follow the "Stage Modifications" notes within each recipe for easy adjustments, such as reducing protein portions or swapping ingredients based on CKD stage.

- **CKD Stage Chart**: Refer to the CKD Stage Nutritional Guide in the meal plan for an overview of protein, potassium, sodium, and fluid recommendations for each CKD stage.

This guide is designed to helps you navigate the meal plan with confidence, knowing you can easily adapt recipes to meet your specific dietary needs at any stage of CKD.

Batch Cooking Tips for Kidney-Friendly Meal Prep

Batch cooking is a great way to save time, reduce stress, and ensure that you always have nutritious, kidney-friendly meals ready throughout the week. This approach involves preparing and storing meals in advance, so you don't have to cook from scratch every day. by focusing on kidney-safe ingredients, you can make meal prep work with your dietary needs. Here's a guide to making the most out of batch cooking and freezer storage.

Make-Ahead Meals for the Week

Preparing meals for the week starts with smart planning and some helpful techniques. Here are some tips to simplify batch cooking while keeping it kidney-friendly:

- **Pre-chop ingredients**: Spend time pre-chopping vegetables and storing them in airtight containers to keep them fresh. This way, you have chopped vegetables ready to use, whether you're making a stir-fry or a salad. For kidney health, choose lower-potassium vegetables like bell peppers, green beans, and cucumbers.

- **Marinate Proteins**: If your meal plan includes proteins like chicken, fish, or tofu, marinate them in kidney-safe spices ahead of time. This step not only adds flavor but also reduces prep time on cooking day. Use seasonings low in sodium, such as fresh herbs, lemon juice, and garlic.

- **Smart Spice Choices**: Use kidney-friendly herbs and spices to enhance flavor without adding sodium. Fresh or dried options like parsley, rosemary, basil, and cumin can keep your meals tasty while meeting kidney diet guidelines.

Storage Instructions

proper storage keeps your prepped ingredients fresh and safe to eat:

- **Use the Right Containers**: store ingredients in glass or BPA-free plastic containers with airtight seals to keep vegetables, proteins, and grains fresh. For extra freshness, use separate containers for each ingredient to prevent flavors from blending together.

- **Refrigeration Tips**: Pre-chopped vegetables and marinated proteins can typically last in the fridge for about 3-5 days. Label each container with the date it was prepped to keep track of freshness.

Batch Cooking Schedules

Organizing your cooking day can help make batch cooking more efficient. Here's a simple schedule to follow on batch-cooking day:

1. **Step 1 - Start with Proteins**: Begin by marinating and cooking proteins, like chicken or tofu, that can be stored and reheated.

2. **Step 2 - Chop Vegetables**: While proteins cook, chop vegetables and store them in containers.

3. **Step 3 - Prepare Grains**: Cook grains, like rice or quinoa, in large batches and store them for quick meals.

4. **Step 4 - Assemble Salads or Snacks**: Put together salads or kidney-friendly snacks that are easy to grab throughout the week.

This sequence helps you get everything prepped efficiently without crowding your kitchen space or losing track of steps.

Freezer-Friendly Dishes

Freezing meals is another excellent way to simplify kidney-friendly meal prep. Freezer meals are convenient for days when you don't have time to cook but still need a healthy, kidney-safe option.

- **Ideal Freezer Meals for CKD**: Some kidney-friendly meals, like soups, stews, and cooked proteins, freeze well and can be reheated without losing flavor. Stick to recipes with low-sodium, low-potassium ingredients for safe storage.

Portioning for CKD Stages

Depending on your stage of CKD, you may need different portion sizes. When freezing, portion out meals in appropriate sizes for each stage:

- **Stage 1-2**: Moderate portions of proteins and vegetables, with careful attention to sodium.
- **Stage 3-4**: Smaller portions of proteins, with even lower sodium levels.
- **Stage 5**: Very low-protein meals, with minimal portions of high-potassium vegetables.

Label each container with the appropriate stage if you're storing for multiple CKD stages in the same freezer.

Best Storage Containers and Labels

- **Freezer Containers**: Choose freezer-safe containers like BPA-free plastic, glass with lids, or reusable silicone bags. They help prevent freezer burn and keep meals fresh longer.

- **Labeling Tips**: Always label each container with the meal name, date, and any specific instructions (e.g., "Stage 4 - Low Protein"). This helps you keep track of what's inside and when it should be used.

Freezing Techniques

- **Cool Before Freezing**: Let meals cool to room temperature before freezing. This prevents ice crystals from forming, which helps retain flavor and texture.
- **Portion into Single Servings**: Freeze in individual portions for easy reheating and to avoid waste.

With these batch cooking and freezer tips, you'll have delicious kidney-friendly meals ready all week, making it easier to stick to your health goals.

Chapter 10: CAREGIVER TIPS AND SUPPORT FOR FAMILY MEMBERS

Supporting a loved one through chronic kidney disease is both a challenge and a privilege—a journey that tests your patience, creativity, and love. This chapter shares some of the ways I was able to support my wife as she navigated the new challenges of her diagnosis. From adjusting our meals to educating family members and friends, every small effort contributed to a greater sense of togetherness and, ultimately, her well-being.

How I Supported My Wife with Kidney Disease

When my wife was first diagnosed, it felt overwhelming for both of us. The dietary restrictions, frequent doctor's visits, and lifestyle adjustments were difficult to process. But as I began to learn more about CKD, I realized that my role as her partner could make a profound difference. I decided to approach this challenge with love, patience, and encouragement, hoping to ease the journey for her.

One of the most effective ways I found to support her was simply through small, consistent acts of encouragement. I started leaving little notes of support on the fridge, reminding her of our goals and how proud I was of her progress. In moments when she felt frustrated by the dietary limitations, I made sure to listen, empathize, and remind her of the progress she was making for her health. Celebrating her victories, no matter how small, helped maintain a positive mindset for both of us.

In the kitchen, I took on the role of chef, becoming more involved in meal planning and preparation. Cooking together became a comforting routine where we explored kidney-friendly recipes and tried new ingredients. It was a way for us to work through the challenges together and find joy in shared meals that supported her health. By making meal prep a team effort, I wanted to show her that she wasn't alone in this journey.

Making Kidney-Friendly Meals for Our Family

Adjusting our meals to be kidney-friendly initially seemed daunting, especially with two children who were used to certain favorite dishes. But rather than making separate meals, I looked for ways to modify our existing recipes so that everyone could enjoy them. For example, I learned how to prepare low-sodium, low-potassium versions of classic dishes and keep additional seasonings on the side for those who wanted them.

One of the most helpful tricks we found was cooking meals "assembly-style." We'd prepare the main components of a meal—like grilled chicken, a variety of vegetables, and low-sodium sauces—and then let everyone build their plate according to their needs. This way, my wife could avoid high-potassium ingredients while the rest of us could add them as desired. over time, this approach became a natural part of our routine, and I noticed that we all benefited from a healthier, more balanced diet.

Finding foods that she loved and could eat safely became a rewarding challenge. For instance, I discovered a way to make low-potassium, creamy mashed potatoes using cauliflower instead. We created kidney-friendly versions of her favorite meals, from pizza with a low-sodium sauce to stir-fries that used her favorite veggies while avoiding potassium-rich ingredients. cooking together was a way to stay connected and create meals that reflected both her dietary needs and her tastes.

Communicating Dietary Needs with Caregivers and Family

One of the unexpected challenges we faced was helping other family members understand her dietary needs. Friends and relatives, who were eager to offer support, often didn't understand why certain foods were off-limits. At family gatherings, I found myself becoming her advocate, politely explaining why she couldn't eat particular dishes and offering simple alternatives that everyone could enjoy.

We decided to create a "CKD-friendly" food guide to share with family members who wanted to support her. The guide included a list of foods that were beneficial for her kidneys and those that could pose a risk. This helped make gatherings easier for everyone, and our family members appreciated knowing how they could help.

When it came to medical appointments or caregivers, I made sure to accompany her, taking notes and asking questions about her dietary needs. Over time, I became fluent in the language of CKD nutrition and could help her communicate her dietary requirements confidently. This also allowed her to feel empowered and supported in situations where it might have been uncomfortable to explain.

Supporting my wife through her journey with CKD has deepened our bond, taught us resilience, and allowed us to grow together in ways we never expected. By embracing the challenges and taking an active role in her care, I've found that what matters most is not just the food on the table but the love, support, and understanding that we share every day. As you move forward in supporting your loved one, remember that your consistent presence, understanding, and effort will mean more to them than words can express.

Chapter 11: GENTLE EXERCISE FOR KIDNEY HEALTH

For anyone managing kidney health, finding ways to stay active can be both empowering and rewarding. When my wife and I first began incorporating exercise into her routine, I quickly realized how much of a positive impact it could have—not only on her physical health but also on her mental well-being. We took it slow, prioritizing movements that were gentle on her body yet effective in promoting circulation, boosting energy, and enhancing overall kidney health. I've seen firsthand how adding low-impact exercises into a daily routine can make a world of difference. If you or a loved one is navigating kidney disease, I want to share these insights to help you reap the benefits of exercise safely and effectively.

Benefits of Exercise for Kidney Health

Exercise is one of the most powerful, natural ways to support your kidneys. Regular, gentle movement promotes heart health, manages weight, and helps control blood pressure—all of which are crucial for maintaining kidney health. Exercise can also reduce stress and improve sleep, which are often overlooked factors that impact kidney function. For my wife, exercise was not only about physical gains; it lifted her spirits, giving her a sense of accomplishment and control over her health.

If you're new to exercise, start small and listen to your body. Even a few minutes of movement each day can help, and over time, you'll likely find yourself feeling more energized, resilient, and ready to take on the journey ahead.

Low-Impact Exercises for Seniors

For those with kidney disease, particularly seniors, low-impact exercises are ideal. These movements are gentle on the joints, minimize strain, and focus on improving balance, flexibility, and strength. Here are a few exercises to consider:

- **Walking:** A simple walk, even if it's around your living room or backyard, is a great way to get moving.

- **Chair Exercises:** Sit on a sturdy chair and try arm raises, leg lifts, or gentle stretches. Chair exercises are great for building strength without putting pressure on your joints.

- **Stretching:** Gentle stretches improve flexibility and circulation. Focus on areas like your neck, shoulders, arms, and legs.

- **Water Exercises:** If you have access to a pool, water exercises are fantastic for building strength without stress on the body.

- **Tai Chi or Yoga:** These low-impact practices combine gentle movement with mindful breathing, improving balance and reducing stress.

Sample Weekly Exercise Routine

Below is a sample weekly exercise routine that's easy to follow and can be adjusted to suit your level of comfort. Start slow, and remember to check with your doctor before beginning any new exercise routine.

Day	Activity
Monday	10-15 min gentle walking
Tuesday	Chair exercises (arm raises, leg lifts)
Wednesday	Rest or gentle stretching
Thursday	10-15 min gentle walking
Friday	Stretching or chair yoga
Saturday	Rest or light walking
Sunday	10-15 min gentle walking

Tips for Staying Active Safely

When exercising, prioritize your comfort and safety above all else. Here are some tips to keep in mind:

1. **Start Small:** Begin with a few minutes each day and gradually increase your time as you feel comfortable. Small steps add up over time.

2. **Listen to Your Body:** Avoid any movements that cause pain or discomfort. Exercise should feel good, not painful.

3. **Stay Hydrated:** Drink water before and after your workout, but avoid excessive hydration if advised by your doctor.

4. **Find a Partner:** Exercising with a friend or family member can make it more enjoyable. My wife and

I enjoyed our walks together—it was a way to connect while staying active.

Exercise can be a valuable tool in supporting kidney health, both physically and mentally. By incorporating gentle movement into your routine, you're taking an active role in your well-being and creating habits that support a better quality of life.

Chapter 12: MAINTAINING A POSITIVE MINDSET AND REDUCING STRESS

Managing kidney disease requires more than just physical care—it's also crucial to nurture a healthy mindset. I've seen how stress can take a toll, both mentally and physically. Supporting my wife through her journey, I learned that stress management and mindfulness were just as important as any medical treatment. A positive mindset helped her stay resilient and focused on her well-being, and I hope these strategies will help you or your loved one find peace and strength along the way.

Mindfulness Techniques for Better Health

Mindfulness is a powerful tool that can bring calm and clarity into your life. Practicing mindfulness doesn't have to be complex—it's as simple as paying attention to the present moment without judgment. For example, a few minutes of deep breathing or focusing on your senses can reduce stress and help you feel grounded. Here are some mindfulness techniques to try:

- **Deep Breathing:** Sit comfortably and take slow, deep breaths, inhaling through your nose and exhaling through your mouth. Focus on the sensation of your breath.

- **Body Scanning:** Lie down and mentally scan your body from head to toe, relaxing each muscle group as you go.
- **Mindful Walking:** If you're on a walk, pay attention to each step and how your body feels as you move. Notice the sights, sounds, and smells around you.

Managing Stress for Kidney Wellness

Chronic stress can impact kidney health by raising blood pressure and affecting your immune system. Managing stress is essential for anyone with CKD. My wife found that engaging in calming activities like reading, journaling, and listening to music helped keep her spirits up. Find what brings you joy and make time for it every day. Small acts of self-care can help you stay resilient.

Breathing Exercises for Relaxation

Breathing exercises are a simple, effective way to calm the mind and body. Here's a quick exercise you can try:

1. **4-7-8 Breathing:** Inhale through your nose for a count of 4, hold for 7, and exhale through your mouth for a count of 8.
2. **Box Breathing:** Inhale for 4, hold for 4, exhale for 4, and pause for 4 before inhaling again. This rhythm can reduce stress and help you feel centered.

Staying Motivated on Your Kidney Health Journey

Staying motivated through the ups and downs of kidney disease isn't always easy. On tough days, my wife and I found comfort in small accomplishments and celebrated every bit of progress. Surround yourself with supportive people, track your achievements, and remind yourself of your goals. Staying motivated is about finding meaning and joy in each step, no matter how small.

A positive mindset and low-stress lifestyle are vital to your health journey. By incorporating mindfulness, relaxation, and gratitude into your routine, you're not only supporting your kidneys but also cultivating resilience and peace within.

Kidney Diet Myths That Could Be Harming You

When it comes to managing kidney health, one of the most challenging aspects is cutting through the noise of misinformation. Everywhere you turn, from the internet to well-meaning friends, there are diet tips, restrictions, and cautionary tales. Unfortunately, many of these common beliefs can be more harmful than helpful.

Here are 7 Common Misconceptions:

Myth #1: "All Protein is Bad for the Kidneys"

For those with kidney disease, it's easy to assume that avoiding protein is a good move, as the kidneys work harder to filter out the waste products from protein breakdown. But the truth is more nuanced. While it's true that excessive protein intake can put a strain on the kidneys, eliminating protein altogether isn't necessary—and can even be harmful.

Research shows that the right amount of high-quality protein, in controlled portions, is vital for maintaining muscle mass, supporting immune function, and keeping up your overall energy. Lean proteins like chicken, turkey, eggs, and certain fish can be safe in moderation, even for people with kidney disease. The key is to work with your healthcare provider to determine the protein amount that best suits your individual needs, rather than avoiding it altogether.

Myth #2: "Low Potassium Means Avoiding All Fruits and Vegetables"

When you're told to limit potassium, it can feel like you need to avoid all fruits and vegetables. Many people believe that "low potassium" translates to a total elimination of nutrient-rich, colorful foods. However, this approach isn't just restrictive; it can also deprive you of essential vitamins and minerals.

The reality is that there are numerous fruits and vegetables that are low in potassium and safe to enjoy. Options like apples, grapes, berries, green beans, and cauliflower are all kidney-friendly. Additionally, portion control plays a significant role. Often, it's not about eliminating potassium altogether but managing it wisely. Knowing which produce items are lower in potassium and keeping portions in check allows you to benefit from these foods without compromising your kidney health.

Myth #3: "Sodium Only Matters if I Have High Blood Pressure"

It's a common misconception that sodium should only be a concern if you have high blood pressure. While reducing sodium intake is a well-known strategy for managing blood pressure, it also has a direct impact on kidney health. Excess sodium can lead to fluid retention, making the kidneys work even harder and potentially causing damage over time.

Limiting sodium intake is essential for everyone managing kidney disease, not just those with high blood pressure. Small changes, like choosing fresh over processed foods and seasoning meals with herbs and spices instead of salt, can make a big difference in your sodium intake and help protect your kidneys.

Myth #4: "All Kidney Diets are the Same"

Many people assume that one-size-fits-all when it comes to kidney diets. In reality, dietary needs vary significantly depending on your kidney disease stage, other health conditions, and personal health factors. This misconception can lead individuals to follow generic advice that may not be right for their specific situation.

A customized approach is the most effective way to support kidney health. A diet that works well for someone with early-stage kidney disease will likely differ from what is best for someone with advanced CKD. By working with your healthcare team, you can create a plan tailored to your specific needs, allowing you to support your health without unnecessary restrictions.

Myth #5: "All Fats Are Bad for Kidneys"

In the quest to eat healthier, some people with kidney disease believe they should cut out fats entirely. While it's true that certain types of fats, like saturated and trans fats, can be harmful to overall health (including kidney health), not all fats are created equal. Healthy fats play an essential role in the body, providing energy, supporting cell function, and aiding in the absorption of vitamins.

For kidney-friendly fat options, focus on unsaturated fats, which can be found in foods like olive oil, avocados, nuts (in moderation), and fatty fish like salmon. These fats are beneficial in small portions and can even help reduce inflammation, which is beneficial for kidney health. Avoid processed foods and trans fats, which can increase the risk of cardiovascular issues and place additional strain on the kidneys. Remember, healthy fats can be part of a balanced diet—just be mindful of portion sizes and types of fat to get the most benefit without compromising kidney health.

Myth #6: "I Need to Drink as Much Water as Possible"

Hydration is essential, but a common myth is that drinking a large amount of water is universally beneficial for kidney health. For those with healthy kidneys, staying hydrated is crucial, but for people with kidney disease—particularly in advanced stages—drinking excessive amounts of water can actually be dangerous. As kidney function declines, the kidneys may struggle to balance fluids, and excess water can lead to swelling, high blood pressure, and a condition called fluid overload, where the body retains too much fluid.

The right amount of water intake varies greatly depending on the stage of kidney disease and other individual health factors. Your healthcare provider can help determine a safe daily fluid allowance based on your kidney function. It's often recommended to avoid "forcing" extra water and instead monitor thirst and follow medical guidance on fluid limits to avoid complications. This myth highlights the importance of individualized hydration strategies for people with kidney disease.

Myth #7: "Herbal Supplements and 'Detox' Teas Will Support Kidney Health"

With the rise in popularity of herbal supplements and detox teas, many people believe these products can "cleanse" the kidneys or improve kidney function. Unfortunately, there is little scientific evidence to support these claims, and in some cases, these products may even be harmful to people with kidney disease. Some herbal supplements contain compounds that can stress the kidneys, and certain detox teas include ingredients that may increase the risk of dehydration or interact with medications used to manage kidney disease.

It's essential to be cautious about supplements or detox products marketed as "kidney cleansers." Always consult a healthcare professional before starting any new supplement regimen, as certain herbs and compounds can exacerbate kidney problems or interfere with prescribed treatments. A true kidney-supportive approach focuses on balanced nutrition, proper hydration, and medically-approved treatments rather than over-the-counter supplements or teas promising quick fixes.

Final Thoughts

Embracing a kidney-friendly diet doesn't mean giving up enjoyable meals or feeling restricted. With the myths debunked and practical guidance laid out, you're now equipped to take control of your health. As you continue through this book, remember that even small changes can yield big improvements over time. Eating well with kidney disease is not only possible; it can be both satisfying and empowering.

CONCLUSION

As you reach the end of this journey through kidney health, I hope you feel equipped with practical tools, comforting support, and encouragement to embrace a healthier lifestyle. My wife's journey with chronic kidney disease taught us both how resilience, knowledge, and care can transform even the toughest challenges into manageable steps forward. I wanted to create a resource that would make this path easier for you—providing clear guidance for kidney-friendly nutrition, gentle exercises, stress management, and a positive mindset.

Remember, every choice you make has the power to support your well-being and bring hope to your journey. Take things one day at a time, celebrate each step forward, and stay connected with those who care about you. As you apply what you've learned here, I hope it brings peace, health, and strength to you and your loved ones.

Thank you for letting me be a part of your journey.

With sincere wishes for your health,

Matthew Brooks

About the Author

Matthew Brooks is a devoted husband and advocate for kidney health, inspired by his wife's journey with chronic kidney disease. Over the years, he has poured his heart into researching ways to support kidney health, including diet, gentle exercise, and stress management. Driven by a desire to make the complex world of kidney care understandable and accessible, Matthew wrote this book to share his insights and experiences with others facing similar challenges.

Matthew believes that family support and knowledge are the foundations of a healthy life. He enjoys spending time with his wife and children, creating kidney-friendly recipes, and staying active through the gentle exercises he has designed for kidney health. His mission is to help others navigate their own health journeys with clarity, compassion, and hope.

Appreciation

To everyone who has supported us along this journey, I am incredibly grateful. To my wife, whose strength inspired this book—thank you for showing me the true meaning of resilience and hope. This book would not exist without your courage.

Thank you to the medical professionals, nutritionists, and fitness experts who generously shared their knowledge and helped shape the resources within these pages. Your dedication to kidney health has transformed lives, and I am honored to incorporate your expertise into this book.

Lastly, to you, the reader—thank you for allowing me to share our story and insights. Your commitment to bettering your health is inspiring, and I wish you continued strength and success on your journey.

Leaving an Honest Review

If this book has helped you on your journey toward kidney health, I would greatly appreciate you leaving an honest review. Your feedback not only helps me improve my work but also supports others who are searching for trustworthy guidance and encouragement in their own lives.

Thank you for taking the time to read and engage with this book. Your experience and thoughts matter, and they can make a difference for others.

With gratitude,

Matthew Brooks

Bonus
Weekly Meal Planner

WEEKLY MEAL PLAN

GROCERY LIST

- MONDAY
- TUESDAY
- WEDNESDAY
- THURSDAY
- FRIDAY
- SATURDAY
- SUNDAY

FROM _____ TO _____

WEEKLY MEAL PLAN

MONDAY

TUESDAY

WEDNESDAY

THURSDAY

FRIDAY

SATURDAY

SUNDAY

GROCERY LIST

FROM _____ TO _____

WEEKLY MEAL PLAN

MONDAY

TUESDAY

WEDNESDAY

THURSDAY

FRIDAY

SATURDAY

SUNDAY

GROCERY LIST

FROM _____ TO _____

WEEKLY MEAL PLAN

MONDAY

TUESDAY

WEDNESDAY

THURSDAY

FRIDAY

SATURDAY

SUNDAY

GROCERY LIST

FROM ___ TO ___

WEEKLY MEAL PLAN

MONDAY

TUESDAY

WEDNESDAY

THURSDAY

FRIDAY

SATURDAY

SUNDAY

GROCERY LIST

FROM _____ TO _____

WEEKLY MEAL PLAN

MONDAY

TUESDAY

WEDNESDAY

THURSDAY

FRIDAY

SATURDAY

SUNDAY

GROCERY LIST

FROM _____ TO _____

WEEKLY MEAL PLAN

MONDAY

TUESDAY

WEDNESDAY

THURSDAY

FRIDAY

SATURDAY

SUNDAY

GROCERY LIST

FROM _____ TO _____

Note

Note

Recipes Index

A
Almond Flour Shortbread Bars   127
Apple and Almond Butter Slices   118
Apple Cinnamon Delight Cups   120
Apple Cinnamon Delight Smoothie   39
Apple Cinnamon Infusion   141
Apple Cinnamon Warm Drink   149
Apple Ginger Fizz   145
Apple Pie Bites   160
Avocado & Cabbage Slaw with Fresh Herbs   58
Avocado and Egg Breakfast Wrap   51

B
Baked Apple Rings with Date Syrup   135
Baked Bananas with Cinnamon   153
Baked Chicken Thighs with Sweet Potatoes & Green Beans 79
Baked Chicken with Rosemary and Lemon   95
Baked Cinnamon Squash Fries   106
Baked Cod with Garlic and Fresh Lemon 87
Baked Pears with Cinnamon and Walnuts 136
Banana Almond Ice Cream   138
Banana-Blueberry Bites   126
Barley & Cucumber Bowl with Lemon-Tahini Sauce 71
Berry & Spinach Salad with Poppy Seed Dressing   56
Berry Almond Butter Smoothie   130
Berry Bliss Smoothie   37
Berry Breakfast Quinoa Bowl   47
Berry Coconut Parfait   119
Berry Quinoa Breakfast Bowl   51
Berry-Ginger Smoothie   148
Blueberry Lemon Sorbet   121
Blueberry Oat Energy Bites   105
Blueberry Orange Bliss   143
Brown Rice & Broccoli Bowl with Miso Dressing 67

C

Cauliflower and Chickpea Stir-Fry   99
Cauliflower Tots   155
Chamomile Honey Tea   150
Chia and Almond Joy Pudding   137
Chia Flax Fiber Porridge   42
Chickpea & Spinach Stew with Turmeric and Cumin   93
Chickpea and Zucchini Pasta with Pesto Sauce   85
Chilled Mango Coconut Sorbet   135
Chilled Pear Compote with Ginger   120
Cilantro Lime Farro & Veggie Bowl   68
Cinnamon Apple Chips   151
Cinnamon Apple Muffins with Oats   123
Cinnamon Apple Quinoa Porridge   41
Cinnamon Carrot Sticks   158
Cinnamon Pear Chips   156
Cinnamon Pear Compote with Agave   134
Cinnamon Spiced Apple Slices   104
Citrus-Glazed Trout with Roasted Asparagus   89
Classic Roasted Red Pepper Hummus   108
Coconut Almond Chia Pudding   53
Coconut Cream Pudding with Maple   131
Coconut Macaroons   152
Coconut Oats Delight   43
Coconut-Lemon Energy Bites   139
Colorful Quinoa & Veggie Medley   56
Comforting Carrot & Cauliflower Soup   59
Cooling Cucumber Mint Water   141
Cranberry Lime Infusion   145
Creamy Peach Smoothie Delight   128
Creamy White Bean and Basil Dip   107
Crisp Cucumber & Herb Salad with Lemon Vinaigrette   55
Crispy Baked Rice with Veggies and a Lemon Vinaigrette   84
Crispy Baked Sweet Potato Fries   114
Crispy Zucchini Chips with Fresh Dill   103
Cucumber and Hummus Sandwiches   75
Cucumber and Tomato Salad   115

Cucumber Avocado Bites   105
Cucumber Kiwi Cool Smoothie   131
Cucumber Lemon Spritzer   148

E
Easy Herb-Crusted Tilapia with Roasted Carrots & Peppers   80
Egg White and Avocado Breakfast Wrap   50
Egg White Salad Wrap with Fresh Dill   65
Egg White Scramble with Spinach and Tomatoes   47
Egg White Veggie Omelette   49
Eggplant Parmesan (Low-Sodium)   97
Eggplant Parmesan with a Fresh Tomato Basil Sauce   92

F
Fiber-Boosted Barley and Vegetable Pilaf   101

G
Garlic and Lemon Cauliflower Mash   101
Garlic Butter Shrimp and Asparagus Sheet Pan   78
Ginger and Pear Delight   143

Ginger Lemon Herbal Tea   150
Ginger-Infused Butternut Squash Soup   61
Green Bean Fries   155
Green Goodness Smoothie   38
Grilled Chicken and Veggie Salad   71
Grilled Pineapple Rings with Coconut Drizzle   122
Grilled Salmon with Asparagus   76
Grilled Salmon with Avocado Salsa   85

H
Heart-Healthy Oatmeal   40
Herbed Chicken & Cucumber Sandwich   65
Herbed Quinoa and Cucumber Salad   100
Herbed Vegetable & Barley Stew   60
Herb-Marinated Grilled Chicken with Spinach and Tomatoes   86
Homemade Guacamole with Veggie Sticks   117
Honey Lemon Sorbet   133
Honey-Sweetened Carrot Loaf   124
Hummus & Veggie Wrap with Crunchy Cabbage   64

K
Kale Chips with Sea Salt 117

L
Lemon and Basil Refreshment 142
Lemon and Garlic Avocado Dip 109
Lemon-Parsley Cauliflower Rice 113
Lentil and Carrot Soup 73
Lentil and Spinach Pasta in a Light Tomato Sauce 83
Low-Potassium Greek Chickpea Salad 57
Low-Sodium Greek Yogurt Herb Dip 110
Low-Sodium Sweet Potato Hash 54

M
Mango Avocado Smoothie 149
Melon Mint Medley Bowl 129
Melon Mint Sparkler 146

N
No-Salt Minestrone Soup 62

O
Oatmeal with Apples and Cinnamon 52
One-Pan Mediterranean Salmon with Olives & Veggies 78

P
Pan-Seared Chicken Breast with Roasted Brussels Sprouts 88
Peach and Lavender Refresher 146
Peach and Yogurt Parfait 53
Pear & Cranberry Crisp 159
Pineapple Coconut Mocktail 147
Pineapple Mint Cooler 144
Pineapple Rings with Honey 153
Poached Eggs on Whole Wheat Toast 49
Pumpkin Chips 159
Pumpkin Spice Cookies 125
Pumpkin Spice Oatmeal 43

Q
Quinoa and Black Bean Veggie Burger Patties 89
Quinoa Avocado Power Bowl 45
Quinoa-Stuffed Bell Peppers with Avocado Dressing 82

R

Raspberry Basil Twist 147
Roasted Carrot and Zucchini Medley 110
Roasted Garlic Cauliflower Bites 116
Roasted Red Pepper & Avocado Sandwich 66

S

Salmon and Veggie Foil Packets 96
Sautéed Green Beans with Shallots 113
Savory Brown Rice with Fresh Herbs 103
Savory Veggie Rice Bowl 44
Simple Sweet Potato & Leek Soup 63
Spiced Peaches 157
Spiced Roasted Sweet Potato Cubes 112
Steamed Broccoli with Garlic and Lemon 111
Strawberry Almond Dream Smoothie 40
Strawberry Avocado Smoothie Bowl 140
Strawberry Bites 158
Strawberry Lime Splash 142
Stuffed Acorn Squash with Brown Rice and Cranberries 90
Stuffed Bell Peppers with Quinoa and Turkey 94
Sweet Potato and Lentil Shepherd's Pie 91
Sweet Potato and Spinach Breakfast Bowl 45

T

Tofu Scramble with Bell Peppers 48
Tropical Mango Berry Bowl 127
Tropical Sunrise Smoothie 38
Turkey & Zucchini Wrap with Lemon Aioli 67
Turkey Lettuce Wraps 74

V

Vanilla Almond Chia Pudding 132
Veggie Nuggets 156

W

Warm Quinoa Bowl with Spinach & Roasted Peppers 69
Watermelon Basil Tonic 144
Whole Wheat Pasta Primavera with Garlic & Olive Oil 81
Wild Rice & Apple Salad with Maple Dressing 70

Z

Zesty Apple and Cabbage Slaw   102
Zesty Herb Cottage Cheese Spread   107
Zesty Lemon Herb Chicken with Roasted Veggies   77

Zucchini and Sweet Potato Fritters   98
Zucchini Fries   154
Zucchini Noodle Bowl   46
Zucchini Noodles with Pesto   72

Made in the USA
Monee, IL
13 March 2025

13956406R00120